Dealer's Choice

'Poker, said David Mamet, is all about character; which is precisely what makes it a perfect dramatic metaphor. It also explains why Patrick Marber's *Dealer's Choice* at the Cottesloe – an outstandingly good first play – is not just about the game itself but also about masculine rituals, the nature of obsession and father-son relationships . . . As movies like *The Cincinatti Kid* long ago realised, any gambling story has a built-in suspense. But Marber's great gift is to use poker not as an end in itself but as a means of exploring character. On a general level, he subtly implies that these are all men who find it difficult to relate to women and who use poker as a sexual substitute.

'More particularly, he explores the nature of compulsion and suggests it is nothing to do with winning or losing: it gradually emerges that the most damaged member of the group is the strictest and most apparently controlled, who uses this Sabbath ritual to fill up the cavernous emptiness in his life.

'What is astonishing in a young, tyro playwright is the absolute control of form: in the pacing of the story and the playing off of one character against another, Marber scarcely puts a foot wrong. It is a hugely promising debut in which Marber throughout plays his own hand with consummate dramatic skill.'

Michael Billington, *Guardian*

Patrick Marber was born in London. *Dealer's Choice* is his first play. It won the *Evening Standard* Award for Best Comedy and the Writers' Guild Award for Best West End Play. He has also written extensively for television and radio, including *After Miss Julie* (BBC Television, 1995).

by the same author

After Miss Julie
Closer

for a complete catalogue of Methuen Drama write to:

Methuen Drama
215 Vauxhall Bridge Road
London SW1V 1EJ

Patrick Marber

Dealer's Choice

Methuen Drama

Methuen Modern Plays

First published in Great Britain in 1995
by Methuen Drama

This revised edition first published in 1996

3 5 7 9 10 8 6 4

Methuen Publishing Limited, 215 Vauxhall Bridge Road,
London SW1V 1EJ

Copyright © 1995, 1996 Patrick Marber
The author has asserted his moral rights

ISBN 0 413 71490 X

A CIP catalogue record for this book
is available from the British Library

Typeset by Wilmaset Ltd, Birkenhead, Wirral
Printed in Great Britain by Cox & Wyman Ltd, Reading, Berks

I would like to thank the following for too many things to mention during the writing of this play: Fiona Bardsley, Jack Bradley, Alan Brodie, Bunny Christie, Chris Colson, Giles Croft, Val Fox, Annoushka Le Gallois, Serena Hill, Mick Hughes, Paul Lyon-Maris, Genista McIntosh, Trish Montemuro, Sarah Overend, Andrew Speed, Nick Starr, Jude Wheway, John Wood and Nicholas Wright.

During the period of November 1993 through to December 1994 *Dealer's Choice* was developed at the Royal National Theatre Studio in the form of rehearsed readings, improvisations and a small-scale production. Without the Studio this play would not exist. I am greatly indebted to the people there: Sue Higginson, Diane Borger, Martin Parker and Lucy Hemmings.

Dealer's Choice was written and rewritten with the help of a number of actors who participated in the many stages of its development: Ross Boatman, Michael Brogan, Matthew Byam-Shaw, Phil Daniels, Perry Fenwick, Kieron Forsyth, Tom Georgeson, Sean Gilder, Cate Hamer, Adam Kotz, Glen Murphy, Steve Nicolson, Ken Oxtoby, Justin Salinger, Stephen Stigwood, Rick Warden and Ray Winstone. David Bark-Jones, Nigel Lindsay and Nicholas Day were present at the first sessions at the Studio right through to the original production at the National and beyond. The characters of Carl, Mugsy and Stephen owe a great deal to their inspiration.

I would also like to thank Richard Eyre who took a risk; he put on an unknown writer's first play at the Royal National Theatre. Furthermore, he let him direct it.

Dealer's Choice is a pessimistic play, a bleak comedy perhaps. I had the time of my life working on it because I had the good fortune to work with these people, here acknowledged.

PM. August 1996.

This play is dedicated to my parents

Dealer's Choice was first presented in the Cottesloe auditorium of the Royal National Theatre, London, on 9 February, 1995. Subsequently, it transferred to the Vaudeville Theatre, presented by Michael Codron. The cast was as follows:

Mugsy	Nigel Lindsay
Sweeney	Ray Winstone
Stephen	Nicholas Day
Frankie	Phil Daniels
Carl	David Bark-Jones
Ash	Tom Georgeson

Directed by Patrick Marber
Designed by Bunny Christie
Lighting by Mick Hughes
Sound by Sue Patrick

This published and final version of the play was presented by the Royal National Theatre in association with the Oxford Playhouse for an international tour in 1996. The cast was as follows:

Mugsy	Kieron Forsyth
Sweeney	Steve Nicolson
Stephen	Nicholas Day
Frankie	Justin Salinger
Carl	Rick Warden
Ash	Ken Oxtoby

Directed by Patrick Marber
Designed by Bunny Christie
Lighting by Mick Hughes and David Boswell
Sound by Sue Patrick

Characters

Mugsy, *a waiter, thirties.*
Sweeney, *a chef, thirties.*
Stephen, *a restaurant owner, late forties.*
Frankie, *a waiter, thirties.*
Carl, *Stephen's son, twenties.*
Ash, *a poker player, early fifties.*

Place
London, England.

Time
A Sunday night and Monday morning in 1996.

Setting
Acts One and Two occur in a kitchen and restaurant.
Act Three occurs in the basement of the same building.

Act One

Early evening.

Stephen *is sitting at a table in the restaurant, drawing.* **Sweeney** *is in the kitchen preparing food.*

Kitchen.

Enter **Mugsy**.

Mugsy   Evening, Sween.

Sweeney   All right, mate.

Mugsy   Hey, Sween, this bloke I know won the lottery.

Sweeney   Oh yeah?

Mugsy   Yeah, he lives on my street. Eight million quid.

Sweeney   Reckon he'll bung you a few?

Mugsy   Nahh, he's a stingy bastard. He's bought a Ferrari. Takes his trouty old mum out for a spin. 'Cept it's up on bricks now, kids nicked the wheels.

Beat.

What I could do with eight million quid . . .

Sweeney   Lose it?

Mugsy   Oh yeah? Call.

Mugsy *tosses a coin.*

Sweeney   Heads.

Mugsy *catches the coin and looks at it . . . heads.*

Mugsy   Bollocks.

He hands the coin to **Sweeney**.

Sweeney   Business as usual.

Mugsy   Here, Sween, what d'you think?

He shows **Sweeney** *his tie.*

Bought it today, thirty quid.

Sweeney   It's very nice.

Mugsy   Yeah?

Sweeney   It's very beautiful.

Mugsy   You taking the piss?

Sweeney *examines the label.*

Sweeney   Ooh, rayon.

Mugsy   What's rayon?

Sweeney   Greek – for rip-off.

Mugsy   They said it was silk. Is rayon made of silk?

Sweeney   All the time.

Mugsy   Good. Is Stephen in?

Sweeney   Next door.

Mugsy   I've got to have words. D'you want to know why?

Sweeney   Not really.

Mugsy   Yes you do, you've got a tell, it's in your eyes. You forget you're dealing with a master of the psychological nuance here. I can read you like the proverbial book.

Sweeney   What 'proverbial' book is that then?

Mugsy   The book of psychological nuance. You OK for tonight?

Beat.

Sweeney   No, not playing.

Mugsy   Hallo?

Sweeney   Goodbye.

Mugsy   What do you mean?

Sweeney   I mean, I'm not playing tonight.

Mugsy   What do you mean, you're not playing?

Sweeney   Is this an exam? I mean, I'm – not – playing – poker – tonight.

Mugsy   But you've got to play, if you don't play we're four-handed, Stephen won't play four-handed, there'll be no game.

Sweeney   I can't play.

Mugsy   We know that.

Sweeney *laughs sarcastically*.

Mugsy   Why can't you play?

Beat.

Sweeney   I'm seeing Louise.

Mugsy   You're seeing a dolly bird?

Sweeney   Louise.

Mugsy   Louise?

Sweeney   My kid, you prat.

Mugsy   I thought your missus wouldn't let you see her?

Sweeney   Well, I'm seeing her tomorrow, special dispensation.

Mugsy   Tomorrow's tomorrow, you can play tonight.

Sweeney   I haven't seen my kid for three months, you could at least pretend to be pleased.

Mugsy (*sarcastic*)   Hurrah.

Sweeney   One dark night some deaf, dumb and blind old hag will spawn *your* child. A stupid, snivelling, scrawny mini Mugsy – then you'll understand responsibility.

Mugsy   And what about your responsibility to poker?

Sweeney   My Louise is more important. I'm not turning up to see her with red eyes, knackered and stinking of booze.

Mugsy   Don't drink then.

Sweeney   I'm sorry if it spoils your evening but that's the way it is. Finito. End of story.

Mugsy   Yeah, cheers.

Beat.

Supposing you win? You could take her somewhere special with the money –

Sweeney   Mugsy –

Mugsy   Madame Tussaud's, the Chamber of Horrors –

Sweeney   Mugsy –

Mugsy   Medieval torture through the ages, kids love that.

Sweeney   SHE'S FIVE.

Pause.

Mugsy   Call.

Sweeney   Why d'you bother?

Mugsy   Just call.

Mugsy *tosses a coin.*

Sweeney   Tails.

Mugsy *looks at it. Tails.*

Mugsy   Bollocks.

He hands **Sweeney** *the coin.*

You seen Carl?

Sweeney   No.

Mugsy   He said he'd come in at six, he promised.

Sweeney   Mr Reliable made you a promise, did he?

Mugsy   He's all right.

Sweeney   He's a ponce.

Mugsy   He's not a ponce.

Sweeney   How much does he owe you?

Beat.

Mugsy Five hundred.

Sweeney Mug.

Beat.

Mugsy I've scrubbed the debt anyway.

Sweeney You done what?

Mugsy Fair's fair, can't have debts . . . between partners.

Sweeney What are you banging on about?

Mugsy If you must know, I'm banging on about a restaurant mate. Me and Carl are going to open a restaurant. French. Maybe Italian. The point is it'll piss all over this place.

Sweeney *You're* going to open a restaurant?

Mugsy Yeah, why not?

Sweeney 'Chez Mugsy'?

Mugsy Oh, very witty.

Sweeney A restaurant with Carl?

Mugsy Stephen dotes on him. He's addicted to him. He'll give us the money to get us started. And then, once we're up and running . . . we dump him.

Sweeney Who, Stephen?

Mugsy No, Carl, we dump Carl.

Sweeney Your partner.

Mugsy It's business.

Sweeney Have you told Stephen about this?

Mugsy No. I'm waiting for Carl to soften him up. Of course, if you were to express an interest, if you were to come and see the premises it might sway Stephen in our favour. I'm talking business, Sween, I'm cutting you in.

Sweeney I'm OK here, Mugs.

Mugsy   Seize the day, grasp the nettle.

Sweeney   Yeah and get stung.

Mugsy   Don't you want to be your own boss?

Sweeney   And I'd be my own boss if I worked for you?

Mugsy   Exactly.

Sweeney   You nipple.

Pause.

So where is this 'restaurant'?

Mugsy   I knew you were interested.

Sweeney   I'm just making conversation.

Mugsy   Yeah, you're like the Invisible Man, completely transparent.

Sweeney   He wasn't transparent.

Mugsy   Course he was, he was invisible.

Sweeney   That's not the same as transparent.

Mugsy   The Invisible Man was invisible, you could see straight through him.

Sweeney   Clingfilm is transparent.

Mugsy   So?

Sweeney   The Invisible Man was not made of clingfilm.

Mugsy   Course he wasn't, he was made of . . . fuck all.

Beat.

Sweeney   So where is this 'restaurant'?

Mugsy   Mile End.

Sweeney   There aren't any restaurants in Mile End.

Mugsy   Exactly.

Sweeney   No one's got any money in Mile End, it's a shithole –

Mugsy   *Used* to be a shithole, now it's 'up and coming'.

Sweeney Says who?

Mugsy Local estate agents, all of them. I've done my research. They say it's highly desirable, desirable people are moving to Mile End in skip loads.

Sweeney Where in Mile End?

Mugsy Mile End Road.

Sweeney It's virtually a motorway.

Mugsy It's a busy main road granted but that's good, plenty of passing trade.

Sweeney Where in the Mile End Road?

Beat.

Mugsy It's a secret. First rule of business, Sween; money first, information later. The premises are in a secret location that I will not disclose until the ink upon the deal is dry.

Sweeney You've lost the plot.

Mugsy I *am* the plot. Look, the point is Stephen is more likely to lend us the money if you've had a look.

Sweeney Rubbish.

Mugsy It's true, he respects you.

Sweeney He respects you too.

Mugsy Does he?

Sweeney Course he does.

Mugsy You reckon?

Sweeney Course.

Mugsy I respect him.

Sweeney He respects you.

Mugsy He does, doesn't he. You're right. Yeah . . . maybe I'll have a quick word with him now . . . sow the germ in his mind . . .

Sweeney You do that, Mugs, good idea.

Mugsy   You'll see.

Sweeney   Well, go on then.

Mugsy   I'm going.

He has forgotten to remove his florescent cycle clip.

This is me going, mate, to make my fortune.

Sweeney   Off you go then.

Beat.

Mugsy   How long you been working here?

Sweeney   Same as you, seven years.

Mugsy   Long time . . . seven years . . . itchy. Long time to be in the same place. You see, Sween, the world is divided between winners and losers, between men of vision and men of . . . blindness.

Sweeney *exits.*

Mugsy   Some can stand the heat, others stay in the kitchen.

He realises he is alone in the kitchen.

I think you know what I'm talking about.

He takes out a coin.

Call.

Sweeney (*off*)   Heads.

Mugsy *tosses the coin.*

Sweeney (*off*)   Just leave it on the table.

Mugsy *looks at the coin.*

Mugsy   Bollocks.

He thinks and then puts the coin in his pocket. He exits into
Restaurant.

Pause.

Mugsy   Evening, Stephen.

Stephen   Hallo, Mugsy. (*Seeing the tie.*) My God, what on earth is that?

Mugsy   New tie.

Stephen   I'm afraid you'll have to take it off, it'll frighten the customers.

He returns to his work.

Everything all right?

Mugsy   Oh yes, couldn't be better.

Stephen   Good.

Mugsy   Has Carl been in?

Stephen   Carl?

Mugsy   Your son.

Stephen   I know who he is, Mugsy. No, why?

Mugsy   No reason.

Beat.

Stephen   Are you all right?

Mugsy   Oh yes, I'm very well.

Beat.

Are you?

Stephen   What?

Mugsy   All right.

Stephen   I'm fine thanks.

Mugsy   Good, I'm glad.

Stephen   Good, so am I.

Beat.

I must say I do enjoy these little chats.

Beat.

Are you sure you're all right?

Mugsy   Yeah. No. Well, one thing . . . I've just been talking to Sweeney and he says he's seeing his kid tomorrow and he doesn't want to stay up late so he won't play tonight.

Stephen   Tomorrow's tomorrow, he can still play tonight.

Mugsy   This is unbelievable, this is the same conversation that I had with Sweeney just now. I literally talked your words out of my mouth into his ear.

Stephen   Really?

Mugsy   It's amazing, it's like we've got something between us . . . something . . .

Stephen   Telepathic?

Mugsy   No, bigger word.

Stephen   Telepathical?

Mugsy   No, begins with an 'S'.

Stephen   Sexual chemistry?

Mugsy   No.

Stephen   Sympathy? Synergy? Synchronicity?

Mugsy   Yeah, that's it. That's what we've got.

Stephen   We've got that, have we?

Mugsy   Yeah, loads of it.

Stephen   Good. Mugsy, you've got to help Sweeney out tonight, you know Tony's not here.

Mugsy   Yeah, where is he?

Stephen   Bolton.

Mugsy   Bolton? What's he doing there? Committing suicide?

Stephen   He's at his father's funeral.

Mugsy   Oh . . . what did he die of?

Stephen   He committed suicide.

Mugsy   God, why?

Stephen   Because he lived in Bolton.

Beat.

Of course he didn't, he had a heart attack.

Mugsy   Heart attack . . . it can do that the heart, can't it
. . . attack.

Beat.

Was there much history of death in the family?

Stephen   Yes, it's been a recurrent problem.

Mugsy   Still, life goes on . . .

Stephen   You could start a new religion with profundities
like that.

Mugsy   Yeah. I mean, no – no, I couldn't, don't have the
time.

Stephen   The point is we're short-staffed tonight so give
Sweeney a hand if he needs it.

Beat.

Mugsy   Stephen, can I have a word –

Stephen (*holding up his work*)   What do you think?

Mugsy   Nice, very nice.

Stephen   Do you think it works?

Mugsy   What is it?

Stephen   It's our new logo for the restaurant.

Mugsy   Very nice. So Carl hasn't been in then?

Stephen   No, Carl has not been in, he won't be in until
midnight for the game. Have you got something to tell me
. . . about you and Carl? Mugsy, you can talk to me, you
know.

Mugsy   I know.

Stephen   So talk to me. Come on, I want the truth . . . are
you pregnant?

Mugsy   Pregnant, very good.

Stephen   Well, I'll just have to wait. You've got me all in a tizzy.

Mugsy   Well, that's just it, isn't it, Stephen, you and I, we understand each other . . . we operate on the same level . . . the same circle . . . we're on the same level of circles . . . aren't we?

Stephen   Yes. And could you ask Sweeney to come in?

Mugsy   You'll never persuade him, he's dead set.

Stephen   Well, we'll see.

He goes back to his work. **Mugsy** *hovers.*

Bye.

Mugsy   Yep, bye.

Stephen   It's that way.

Mugsy   Stephen, there is something I'd like to talk to you –

Stephen (*pointing to his watch*)   Mugsy . . .

Mugsy   I'll be going then.

Stephen   And Mugsy . . .

Mugsy   What?

Stephen   Cycle clip.

Mugsy   Cycle clip.

Mugsy *exits into*

Kitchen.

Sweeney *enters as* **Mugsy** *returns.* **Mugsy** *puts on a different tie.*

Mugsy   A man of vision.

Sweeney   You told him?

Mugsy   We had words.

Sweeney   Did you tell him?

Mugsy   Our conversation covered a gamut of topics, restaurantering was but one of them.

Sweeney   So you didn't tell him.

Mugsy   No. He wants to see you.

Sweeney   You didn't tell him I wasn't playing?

Mugsy   Sorry, mate, he prised it out of me.

Sweeney   Cheers, now I get an earful.

Mugsy   Not if you play.

Mugsy *starts to read the paper.*

Sweeney   Oi, the floor needs a mop in there.

Mugsy   It's Frankie's turn. He's late. Probably shagging.

Sweeney   Jealous?

Mugsy   No.

Sweeney *laughs.*

Mugsy   No. Did he pull that blonde bird?

Sweeney   Never you mind.

Mugsy (*wistful*)   She was gorgeous, tits like the Hindenburg. Two Hindenburgs.

Sweeney   Mugsy. Evolve. Floor.

Mugsy   It's Frankie's turn, have a go at him, or don't you want to cos he's your boyfriend?

Sweeney   You're unbelievable –

Mugsy   Well, your missus leaves you –

Sweeney   She didn't leave me, it was mutual –

Mugsy   Yeah, your missus mutually left you, Frankie moves in, tongues will wag –

Sweeney   Tongues will be cut off. Mugsy, do us a favour, mop the floor.

Enter **Frankie**.

Frankie   Evening all.

Mugsy *and* **Sweeney**   All right, mate.

Frankie   Where's Genghis?

Sweeney   Next door, first snoop expected.

Mugsy   Here, Frankie, Sween says he's not playing tonight.

Frankie   I know, no problem.

Mugsy   There won't be a game if he doesn't play, we'll be four-handed.

Frankie   No we won't, there's me, you, Stephen, Carl –

Mugsy   And?

Frankie   Tony.

Mugsy (*triumphant*)   He's at his dad's funeral.

Frankie   Fuck.

Mugsy   Yeah, big fuck.

Sweeney   Look on the bright side, boys, you're not gonna do your bollocks for another week.

Mugsy   I haven't done 'em for quite a long time actually –

Frankie   Not since the . . . since the . . .

Mugsy   Don't –

Sweeney   The –

Frankie   The un –

Mugsy   Don't –

Sweeney   The unment –

Mugsy   Don't –

Frankie   The 'unmentionable'?

Mugsy   Oi.

Beat.

So . . .

Frankie   What?

Mugsy   Did you score?

Frankie   When?

Mugsy   Last night.

Frankie   Who?

Mugsy   The blonde with the hair on table ten.

Frankie   Never you mind.

Mugsy   Go on, did you hit middle pin? Did you fill your straight? Did you flop the nuts?

Frankie   'Fraid not Mugsy . . . but I got a shag.

Mugsy   You're disgusting, you're like a dog on heat.

Frankie   Bitches go on heat, Mugsy.

Mugsy   You should have a test, mate.

Frankie   I passed my cycling proficiency.

Sweeney   No you didn't.

Mugsy   You won't be laughing when you find out you've got HIV. When you get paid back for all your filthiness, you're pox-ridden, you're a walking syringe –

Sweeney   Not in front of the food Mugs.

Mugsy   Your cock is a needle full of death, mate.

Frankie   Well, you know what they say, Mugs; if you're going down you might as well take someone with you.

Frankie *pushes* **Mugsy** *face down on the table and pretends to sodomise him.* **Mugsy** *screams.*

Sweeney   Go on, you Mug, you know you want it.

Frankie *lets* **Mugsy** *free.*

Mugsy   I'm serious, it's irresponsible. I hope you wipe the bog seat after you've been.

Sweeney   Here Frankie, has The Mug told you about his 'pleasure dome'?

Mugsy What 'pleasure dome'?

Sweeney In Mile End.

Frankie What's this?

Mugsy Never you mind.

Sweeney Mugsy's going into the restaurant business.

Frankie Oh yeah? Any chance of a job?

Mugsy You must be joking.

Frankie I think I must.

Sweeney Mugs, tell him where it is.

Mugsy Mile End Road.

Frankie Nice and busy.

Mugsy Exactly, thank you.

Frankie Plenty of local violence, good for atmosphere.

Mugsy You can get stabbed anywhere, nowhere's safe.

Sweeney The question is where is it in the Mile End Road?

Mugsy Never you mind.

Sweeney See, Frankie, that's the big mystery. No one must know the secret location of Mugsy's Masterplan for culinary domination.

Frankie So we'll never know?

Sweeney You will go to your grave not knowing.

Frankie and **Sweeney** (*weeping*) Why won't he tell us? Please, Mugsy tell us where it is.

Mugsy All right, all right. If you must know I'll tell you.
Beat.

Sweeney Too late now, mate.

Frankie You had your chance.

Mugsy No, I *will* tell you but if you tell anyone else –

Frankie What? What you gonna do about it, Tiger?

Mugsy   I'll sue you.

Frankie   Oh right, I won't tell a soul then, Scout's honour.

Mugsy   Sween?

Sweeney   Swear, Brownie's honour.

Mugsy   I'm serious.

Mugsy *illustrates with his tie.*

OK, this is the Mile End Road.

Sweeney   Where's London?

Mugsy   Mile End is in London.

Sweeney   Where's Central London?

Mugsy   It is Central London, it's ten minutes from the West End, it's 'conveniently located'. OK, you know the police station.

Frankie   Yep . . .

Mugsy   Walk up fifty yards, crappy little park on your right.

Sweeney   Yep . . .

Mugsy   Hospital on the left.

Frankie   Yep . . .

Mugsy   You know the public conveniences?

Sweeney   Yep . . .

Mugsy *points as if to rest his case. Pause.* **Mugsy** *points again.*

Sweeney   No . . . no . . . tell me it's not true, Mugsy . . . no . . .

Mugsy   What?

Sweeney   It's a wind-up.

Mugsy   It's a Business Opportunity Scheme, this bloke from the council says I can have them for a grand. It's a grand –

Sweeney   It's a toilet.

Mugsy   They're enormous. It's potential on a stick. Come and see then you'll understand.

Sweeney   I've got a toilet in my flat, it wins prizes, I don't need to see another one.

Mugsy   Yeah yeah, they laughed at the man who invented the wheel.

Sweeney   Who was that then?

Mugsy   I don't know, Mr Fucking Wheel.

Sweeney   Friend of Mr Fire, was he?

Mugsy   Yeah and Mr Toilet.

Sweeney *laughs.*

Mugsy   Yeah, ha ha ha, big joke. Yes, it's a toilet, who cares.

Sweeney   Certainly not lovers of haute cuisine, they travel the world looking for the elusive khazi cum restaurant.

Beat.

Frankie   You say it's the one near the hospital?

Mugsy   Yes . . .

Frankie   I had a piss in there last week. It's very spacious.

Sweeney *continues laughing.*

Frankie   No, Sween. Give the man a chance.

Mugsy   Thank you, Frankie.

Frankie   Don't worry, mate, your secret's safe with us.

Mugsy   Thanks, Frank. I'm glad someone understands.

Frankie   Best of luck, Mugs.

Mugsy   Cheers. Vision, that's all you need.

Frankie   Well, you got to have a dream, haven't you?

Mugsy   Yes you have.

Frankie   And your dream is a toilet in the Mile End Road.

Mugsy   Are you taking the piss?

Frankie   More your line of work by the sound of things.

Mugsy   You're a wanker, Frankie.

Frankie   No I'm not, it's just I'm *jealous* of your visionary perception. See, when I walk past say . . . a graveyard . . . I can't see it as anything other than a graveyard. *You* see a graveyard and think . . . casino. That's the difference between us, Mugs, vision. (*To* **Sweeney**.) I'm going for a smoke.

Frankie *exits*.

Sweeney   What is this?

Mugsy   What?

Sweeney   This.

Mugsy   This what?

Sweeney   This . . . business.

Mugsy   This is me.

Sweeney   This isn't you.

Mugsy   Yes it is.

Beat.

Sweeney   Did you tell Stephen it was a toilet?

Mugsy   Not in so many words.

Sweeney   In any words?

Beat.

Be careful, Mugs.

Mugsy   I am careful, they're a grand, Sween, a grand, if we play tonight I could win a grand easy.

Sweeney   Or lose it.

Restaurant.

Enter **Carl**.

Carl   Hi, Dad.

Stephen   Hallo, Carl. What are you doing here?

Carl   Came to see you.

Stephen   I'll get my cheque book . . .

Carl   I don't need money.

Stephen   Hallelujah.

Carl (*seeing logo*)   That's good.

Stephen   Thank you, it's our new logo, I'm rather proud of it.

Carl   Yeah, it's great. I've got a friend who could artwork that for you.

Stephen   It is artworked, this is it.

Carl   No, I mean do the layout so you can have it printed.

Stephen   This is the layout . . .

Carl   No, I mean . . . d'you want a drink?

Stephen   In other words, 'Can I have a drink, Dad?'

Carl   Yes.

Stephen   While you're there could you tell Sweeney I need a word.

Carl   Sure. Do you want one?

Stephen   No thanks.

Kitchen.

Enter **Carl** *who walks through and off.*

Carl   All right, lads.

Sweeney   All right, Carl.

Mugsy   Carl, Carl, have you told him?

Carl (*off*)   Not yet, I've only just got here.

Sweeney   You playing tonight, Carl?

Carl (*off*)   Yeah.

He emerges with beer bottle.

Sweeney, Dad wants a word when you've got a min

He is leaving. **Frankie** *enters.*

Sweeney   Carl, you got that ton you owe me?

Carl   You said Saturday.

Sweeney   Yeah and today's Sunday.

Carl   No Saturday next week.

Sweeney   This week.

Frankie   You got my fifty?

Carl   What fifty?

Frankie   The fifty quid you owe me.

Carl   I don't owe you fifty, do I?

Frankie   No.

Carl   You just said –

Sweeney   Where is it?

Carl   We said next week.

Sweeney   I need it, Carl.

Beat.

Frankie   What you playing with tonight, Carl?

Carl   Money.

Sweeney   So give me some.

Carl   I haven't got it yet, Sween, I'm sorry.

Sweeney   Well, how are you going to play then?

Frankie   Daddy will provide.

Carl   I'm owed money.

Mugsy   Leave him alone, he's good for it.

Sweeney   From who?

Carl   Tony owes me three hundred.

Beat.

Frankie   He's not here.

Carl   What?

Sweeney   He's at a funeral.

Carl   Where?

Mugsy   Bolton.

Frankie (*helpfully*)   You could get a cab.

Carl   Who died?

Mugsy   His dad, I reckon it's the water up there, it's got bits in it.

Carl   I'll get you your money, Sween, I promise. Trust me.

Sweeney   Why?

Carl   What?

Beat.

Sweeney   Why should I trust *you*?

Pause.

Mugsy   Carl, good luck.

Carl *exits into restaurant.*

Mugsy   Look, if you need it that badly I'll cover it.

Sweeney   Just mop the floor.

Mugsy *exits.*

Restaurant.

Stephen   So . . . how are you?

Carl   Very well.

Stephen   OK for the game?

Carl   Uh huh.

Stephen   Actually, there may not be one. We've got a problem with Sweeney, he's seeing his sprog tomorrow, says he won't play tonight.

Carl   I'm sure you can work on him.

Stephen   How's your mother?

Carl   She's fine.

Stephen   Does she let you call her 'mother' yet or do you still have to call her Claire? And how's the drop-out centre? Sorry, drop-in centre.

Carl   It's a Healing Centre, Dad, they're doing very well, they're nearly in profit.

Stephen   Nearly? Well, I'll be.

Carl   You were a hippy once.

Stephen   Yuh, once.

Beat.

So . . . what do you want?

Carl   I've got a proposition. You know the Mile End Road . . .

Stephen   Wasn't it Eliot's inspiration for *The Wasteland*?

Carl   It's great, it's got character.

Stephen   Ah.

Carl   What do you mean 'ah'?

Stephen   Isn't 'character' a euphemism for ugly?

Carl   Yes, yes it is. Look, Mugsy wants to open a restaurant –

Stephen   He wants to what?

Carl   And he wants me to be his partner.

Stephen   I've heard of the blind leading the blind but –

Carl   Please, Dad. He . . . we need some money, a quick loan, just to secure the premises –

Stephen   What 'premises'?

Carl   The . . . place, in the Mile End Road.

Stephen   What sort of money?

Beat.

Carl   Three thousand pounds.

Kitchen.

Frankie   Sween . . .

Sweeney   Before you start I'm not playing.

Frankie   I know, no problem.

Pause.

Sweeney   So . . . did you give it one or what?

Frankie   'It'?

Sweeney   Blonde bird, Table Ten, well-developed.

Beat.

Frankie   Nahh, she got a cab.

Sweeney   You bullshit merchant.

Sweeney *exits.*

Frankie   We had a fumble.

Restaurant.

Stephen   Do you really want to open a restaurant?

Carl   Yes I do.

Pause.

Stephen   I thought you wanted to be a . . . 'do nothing', we've been through all this.

Carl   Well, I've decided I do want to . . . 'do something'. I can't deliver pizzas all my life.

Stephen   So when did this Damascan conversion occur?

Carl   I don't know. Does it matter? I thought you'd be pleased. You could teach us. I mean, you're right, I have been . . . 'treading water'. Look, can you lend us the money?

Stephen   Carl, I can't lend you this money just like that.

Carl   You could.

Stephen   I'm sorry, it would be irresponsible, I can't just give you and Mugsy three thousand pounds . . . the man's a half-wit. He's still paying me off for the 'unmentionable' and he thinks –

Carl   He thought you might have faith in him – and me – he thought in his innocence you might actually *want* to invest in him –

Stephen   Invest in him? What, as a tax write-off? The man's a cretin.

Carl   He's not a cretin, Dad.

Stephen   He's a bloody idiot.

Carl   Fine. Just let him down gently, don't do a number on him.

Stephen   What do you mean 'do a number on him'?

Carl   Just don't abuse him.

Stephen   Has he got any idea what it costs to –

Carl   I'm sure he's got no idea.

Pause.

Stephen   Look, Carl, I'm sorry, I do appreciate your desire to . . . if you worked here and learnt the business properly then maybe –

Carl   There's no point, it's not going to happen so –

Stephen   No, I don't mean work for me, I mean work *with* me. I'd like that, Carl, I'd like to see you more than once a week for a game of cards.

Carl   I've worked here before, it doesn't work.

Kitchen.

Sweeney (*entering*)   D'you do the washing up?

Frankie   Sorry. I'll do it soon as I get home.

Sweeney   I'll be home first.

Pause.

How come you're so late?

Frankie   Never you mind.

Sweeney   How come you're so late?

Frankie   Been to the travel agent.

Sweeney   Oh yeah? Booking a dirty weekend – alone – what is it, 'Wanker's Package'?

Frankie   Never you mind.

Restaurant.

Stephen   But you're OK for tonight? You are OK for the game?

Carl   Not exactly, I've got a cashflow problem. Tony owes me money.

Stephen   Tony's not here.

Carl   I know.

Kitchen.

Frankie   So you're seeing Louise.

Sweeney   Yeah.

Frankie   That's good.

Sweeney   Yeah.

Frankie   What time?

Sweeney   Nine.

Frankie   Early.

Sweeney   Yeah, we're going to the zoo, Mugsy suggested the Chamber of Horrors.

Frankie   She's only six.

Sweeney   Five.

Beat.

Frankie   Yeah, but it's her birthday soon, isn't it?

Sweeney   Last month.

Restaurant.

Stephen   So . . . are you saying you want me to lend you the money for the game?

Carl   No I'm not, I haven't got the money so I won't play.

Stephen   I don't believe this, first Sweeney cries off, now you. I've been organising poker games for the best part of twenty years, I've never had such trouble getting a game together.

Kitchen.

Frankie   So what time does the zoo open?

Sweeney   I dunno, ten? Eleven?

Frankie   Gonna spend all day there? I mean, kids get bored easy, don't they.

Sweeney   Louise loves animals.

Frankie   Take Mugsy.

Sweeney   Nahh, he'd frighten the gorillas.

Restaurant.

Stephen   If you don't play how are you ever going to learn?

Carl   Learn what?

Stephen   Self-discipline.

Carl   Poker's got nothing to do with self-discipline. It's about guts, it's about risk, it's about passion –

Stephen   You're living in a fantasy world Carl, you're not the Cincinnati Kid.

Kitchen.

Frankie   Be a shame not to play.

Sweeney   Frank, don't guilt-trip me.

Restaurant.

Stephen   Carl, poker is all about discipline. The discipline of the game itself and the discipline of turning up here every Sunday night with a hundred pounds to play in the game.

Carl   It's not school.

Stephen   It is actually, it's a poker school.

Kitchen.

Sweeney   What is this? Don't you understand I've got no choice.

Frankie   Course you've got a choice. You can play cards *and* see your kid.

Sweeney   Her name's Louise. I want to be awake when I see my daughter. I don't want to be sulking about some pot I lost when she's looking at the . . . penguins all excited.

Restaurant.

Stephen   Carl, I taught you everything you know about poker.

Carl   I do OK . . .

Stephen   What about last week? You played like a mug, you outmugged Mugsy which is saying something.

Kitchen.

Frankie   Do you want to play?

Sweeney   Course I want to play.

Frankie   So stop pretending to be 'el perfecto daddyo' and play.

Restaurant.

Carl   OK, last week I lost but usually, this year, I've been winning.

Stephen   I'm sorry, Carl, you're wrong. I log every game, remember? You're losing.

Kitchen.

Frankie   You scared of losing?

Sweeney   No.

Restaurant.

Carl   It depends where you take the log from.

Stephen   You're losing.

Kitchen.

Sweeney   Yeah, all right, I'm scared of losing. I've done a grand the last three weeks, supposing I do all my dough tonight and then I've got nothing to spend on Louise tomorrow?

Frankie   Stick fifty quid in your back pocket, don't touch it.

Sweeney   I haven't got the discipline.

Restaurant.

Stephen   You've got no discipline, you bet when you should check, you call when you should – you play like a girl.

Carl   Well, you taught me.

Kitchen.

Frankie   You taught me how to play.

Sweeney   That was at school, Frank, it was years ago.

Frankie   So?

Restaurant.

Stephen   Well, then either I taught you badly or maybe, Carl . . . you don't learn.

Kitchen.

Sweeney   So . . . now you're a better player than me, all right.

Restaurant.

Stephen   Carl, why can't you –

Carl   What, be like you?

Kitchen.

Frankie   Lost your bottle? Gone soft?

Sweeney   There's no shame in being scared.

Frankie   There is at a poker table.

Sweeney   We're not at a poker table.

Restaurant.

Stephen   You can't spend your whole life borrowing money.

Kitchen.

Frankie   Sweeney Ted?

Sweeney   Yeah 'Sweeney Ted'.

Restaurant.

Carl   If it's so important that I play I'll borrow the money off mum.

Stephen   Don't bring her into this.

A series of intercuts between the two rooms.

Frankie   Come on, Sween.

Stephen   This is about you and me.

Carl   I thought it was about poker.

Frankie   Come on, Sween.

Sweeney   Drop it, Frankie.

Stephen   Your mother –

Frankie   You wanker –

Stephen   When I was your age I was supporting a family . . .

Sweeney   Go fuck yourself.

Stephen   While your mother sat at home on her fat buddhist arse . . .

Frankie   Cunt.

Stephen   With a feeding bottle in one hand . . .

Sweeney   You're the cunt.

Stephen   And a joint in the other.

Carl   So fucking what.

Improvised row sequence at full volume lasting about twenty seconds until **Mugsy** *marches into the kitchen carrying a mop and bucket.*

Sweeney   FUCK OFF, MUGSY.

Mugsy *exits into restaurant.*

Stephen (*to* **Mugsy**)   Out.

Mugsy *exits back into kitchen.*

Sweeney   FUCK OFF, MUGSY.

Mugsy   I am fucking off.

Mugsy *fiddles with the mop trying to get it to stand up against a chair.*

Stephen   Come and sit down, Carl.

Carl   Don't shout at me.

Sweeney   WELL, FUCK OFF THEN.

Carl   I don't have shouting, Dad.

Mugsy   This is me fucking off, all right.

Stephen   DON'T BE SUCH A FUCKING LITTLE MADAM AND COME AND SIT HERE.

Carl   No shouting.

Stephen (*shouting*)   ALL RIGHT.

Sweeney   FUCK OFF NOW.

Carl   No shouting.

Mugsy   I'm fucking off, I'm fucking off.

Sweeney   SO FUCK OFF THEN.

Mugsy *exits.*

Stephen (*shouting*)   All right, please just come and sit down and talk to me. Please, Carl, let's sit down and talk about this in a civilised fashion.

Pause.

Mugsy (*off*)   I've fucked off.

Restaurant.

Stephen   Look, you have to understand I can't keep lending you –

Carl   But that's not it, Dad –

Stephen   Will you just once, just once, let me finish a sentence.

Kitchen.

Sweeney   I'm not playing, all right.

Frankie   All right, you're not playing, fine.

Restaurant.

Carl   Why does it have to be so emotional? Why can't it be like you're a bank and I'm a customer?

Stephen   But, Carl –

Carl   So there's no emotional ties, so it's outside us, so it's just a transaction –

Stephen   How dare you, if you want money from a bank you go to a fucking bank.

Carl   I can't go to a bank.

Stephen   And why is that, Carl? Because you were a compulsive gambler, Carl. Because you were addicted to slot machines, which, by the way, is the most ridiculous thing I've ever heard in my entire life. No bank will touch you, Carl, because last year you were bouncing cheques all over London and your father, your father the bastard, i.e. me (by the way) covered all your debts so that you wouldn't go to prison.

Carl   I wouldn't have gone to prison.

Stephen Yes you would. So don't call me a bank, don't for one second think there can be any 'transaction' between us that isn't emotional because whether you like it or not I am your father and you are my son.

Kitchen.

Frankie D'you want a drink?

Sweeney Yeah, go on, open a bottle of house red.

Frankie *exits.*

Restaurant.

Carl Just because *you're* successful doesn't mean that I –

Stephen Successful?

Carl Yes you are, you've built this place up from nothing.

Stephen Do me a favour, don't come in here spouting your naive olde worlde bollocks, 'Ee, Dad, you built this oop from nowt.' Who gives a fuck.

Pause.

(*Calm.*) I want you to play, Carl. If you don't play I don't see you.

Pause.

Don't you understand? It's blackmail.

Pause.

Carl No it's not. Look, I haven't got the money so I won't play. See you next week.

Carl *walks to exit.*

Stephen Here you are . . . one hundred pounds.

He holds up the cash. **Carl** *turns to exit.*

Please . . . Carl . . .

Silence.

Carl (*taking the money*) I'm sorry.

Beat.

If I win tonight I'll pay it back tonight. OK?

Stephen   OK.

Carl   See you later.

Carl *exits.*

Silence.

Kitchen.

Frankie *returns with a bottle of red wine. He pours* **Sweeney** *a glass.*

Frankie   More tea, vicar?

Sweeney   Bless you, my son. (*Drinking.*) What's this?

Frankie   House red.

Sweeney   Bollocks, show me.

Frankie *shows him the label.*

Sweeney   Frankie, this is forty quid a bottle.

Frankie   The house has decided to drink *good* red tonight.

Sweeney   On your head, Frankie.

Frankie   Ooo, I'm so scared . . . Sweeney Ted.

Sweeney   Watch it. Where's Mugsy?

Frankie   Downstairs, playing patience, poor sod. He was cheating. Can't even win at patience.

Sweeney   I'm worried about him.

Frankie   Aren't we all.

Sweeney   No, I mean about his toilet.

Frankie   Chateau Mugs? Bottoms up.

Sweeney   He's serious, you know, I mean, Stephen ain't gonna give him no money.

Frankie   He won't give him a winkle.

Enter **Mugsy**.

Mugsy   Can I come in?

Frankie   You are in.

Mugsy Yeah, but I mean, shall I go?

Sweeney No, grab a chair and have a drink. I'm sorry. For shouting. I'm a cunt.

Mugsy S'all right.

Frankie *begins to pour* **Mugsy** *a glass of wine.*

Frankie Here you go.

Mugsy No thanks, you know I don't like wine . . .

Beat.

Here, boys, that's an idea, I might make my restaurant teetotal . . . quite a good angle . . . might get us some publicity. What d'you reckon, Sween?

Sweeney Yeah, good idea.

Frankie (*picking up the mop*) I'll do that, Mugsy.

Mugsy Are you sure?

Frankie Yeah.

Mugsy Cheers. (*To* **Frankie**.) Shall I do it now?

Frankie Yeah, go on, have a go.

Frankie *exits into restaurant and begins to mop the floor.*

Mugsy So . . . Frankie didn't persuade you to play?

Sweeney 'Fraid not, Mugsy.

Mugsy Yeah, I'd be the same if I had a kid. Or I'd teach my kid to play, like Stephen did.

Beat.

It's a shame really 'cos tonight . . . was going to be my last game.

Sweeney You what?

Mugsy Yeah, I had a medical this afternoon and . . . the doctor says I can't play no more . . . I've got this rare heart condition . . . it can't stand the excitement . . . so that's it

. . . no more poker . . . I've lost my greatest love . . . I'll get over it I s'pose . . . in time.

He sobs.

Sween?

Beat.

Sweeney   Is that the best you can do?

Mugsy   Yeah, I think it is.

Sweeney   You doughnut.

Mugsy   Go on, Sween, play. Go on. Play for me, please, Sween, for me, play for me, please, Sween, play. I feel lucky tonight, I feel lucky for you tonight. Play.

Sweeney   All right, if it makes *you* happy, I'll play.

Mugsy   Good man.

Sweeney   For an hour.

Mugsy   Good man.

Enter **Stephen**.

Stephen   Sweeney, have any of my messenger boys asked you to come and see me?

Mugsy   It's all right, he's playing.

Stephen (*to* **Sweeney**)   Are you?

Sweeney   Yes.

Stephen   Excellent.

Mugsy   I used my unique persuasive powers and he crumbled instantaneously.

Stephen   Good for you.

Mugsy   So did Carl have a word with you?

Stephen   Yup.

Mugsy   And are you chomping at the proverbial bit?

Stephen   I'm positively tumescent, Mugsy, but can we discuss it later? We're opening.

Mugsy We certainly can. Prior to the game we shall thrash out the deal and then I will castrate you.

Beat.

With my poker sword. (*To* **Sweeney**.) And you.

Sweeney Oh yeah?

Mugsy *exits into restaurant.*

Stephen Cycle clip.

Sweeney Stephen, is it OK to take the lamb off, we've only got one left?

Stephen Fine, sacrifice it.

Beat.

Sween, have you heard about Mugsy's 'scheme'?

Sweeney Yeah, it's been mentioned.

Stephen What the hell am I going to say to him? I can't possibly lend him any money.

Sweeney I know. Tell him straight.

Beat.

Stephen I'm glad you're playing, Sweeney.

Sweeney Well, I couldn't let you down, boss.

Stephen (*showing him the logo*) Hey, what do you think of this? New logo.

Sweeney *examines it.*

Sweeney Nahh, don't like it.

Sweeney *exits.* **Stephen** *exits into*

Restaurant.

Stephen Gentlemen, to work. Frankie, fix the wobble under that table, will you.

Frankie Yeah.

Stephen 'Yes' is the word.

Frankie   Yes.

Mugsy   There'll be no wobbly tables in my place.

Stephen   No, just wobbly waiters. (*Showing logo.*) Frankie, what do *you* think of –

Stephen *realises it's not worth it, he screws up his logo and throws it on the floor.*

Mugsy . . . rubbish.

Mugsy   Yes, boss.

Stephen   And Mugsy . . . cycle clip.

Mugsy   Yeah, cycle clip, cycle clip.

Mugsy *removes his cycle clip forgetting to pick up the rubbish.*

Stephen   Mugsy . . . rubbish.

Mugsy   Toss you for it.

Stephen   No.

Mugsy *clucks 'chicken'.*

Stephen   Oh . . . all right.

Mugsy *tosses a coin.*

Stephen   Heads.

Mugsy *looks at the coin.*

Mugsy   Yes. Tails it is. Go on, my son.

Stephen *picks up the rubbish.*

Mugsy   I told you, this is my night. The Mug Is On A Roll.

Act Two

Midnight.

The restaurant is closed. One customer, **Ash**, *remains seated at a table.* **Stephen** *and* **Mugsy** *are in the restaurant.*

Kitchen.

Frankie   Another bottle?

Sweeney   Yeah, why not.

Exit **Frankie**.

Restaurant.

Mugsy *approaches* **Ash**'s *table.* **Stephen** *exits into kitchen.*

Mugsy   Would you like some coffee?

Ash   Please. Cappuccino.

Mugsy   Ah, no, sorry, the machine's broken. Italian. We've got filter or instant, same thing really.

Ash   What is?

Mugsy   Filter and instant. I can't taste the difference, can you? Same with wine. I mean, obviously I can taste the difference between red and white . . . I mean white's sourer, isn't it? But red and red, it all tastes red to me. Then again I prefer Tango.

Ash   I'll have filter.

Mugsy   Filter, right you are. It's a cafetière actually, it's a jug with a plunger.

Ash   Sounds great. And a couple of Amaretti biscuits as well.

Mugsy   I'm sorry?

Ash   Amaretti biscuits. You know, with the paper, you burn them.

Mugsy   You burn the biscuits?

Ash   No, the paper. You set fire to the paper and it goes up.

Mugsy   Why?

Beat.

Ash   Physics.

Mugsy   Right, where would we be without physics? Probably upside down or floating. Actually, I meant why do you set fire to the paper?

Ash   For fun . . . it's fun.

Mugsy   I'll go and see if we've got any.

Mugsy *exits into*

Kitchen.

Stephen   Come on, Mugs.

Mugsy   It's not my fault.

Stephen   What does he want?

Mugsy   Coffee.

Stephen   Well, serve him his coffee and then with all the subtlety you can muster ask him if he wants his bill.

Mugsy   Why?

Stephen   Because I'd quite like to start a poker game this century.

Mugsy   It's rude to hurry people.

Stephen   Well, when you're running your establishment in the Mile End Road you can let your punters linger in the post-riot after-glow all night. Meanwhile, please get rid of him.

Stephen *goes back into the restaurant.*

Mugsy   Have we got any . . . of those biscuits that go on fire?

Sweeney *looks at him.*

Restaurant.

Stephen *approaches* **Ash**'s *table.*

Stephen   Everything all right?

Ash   Yeah, thanks.

Stephen   You enjoyed your meal?

Ash   Not really, no.

Stephen   I'm sorry, why was that?

Ash   My steak wasn't cooked and it was cold.

Stephen   Which steak did you order?

Beat.

Ash   Steak tartare.

Kitchen.

Frankie *returns with another bottle of wine.*

Frankie   More vino, Sweeno.

Sweeney   Cheers.

They drink.

So when you going on this holiday?

Frankie   Soon.

Sweeney   Who you going with?

Frankie   On me tod. I'm a big boy now.

Sweeney   I could do with a holiday . . .

Frankie   Better win tonight then, hadn't you?

Restaurant.

Stephen   Anything else we can get you before we close?

Ash   I asked for some Amaretti biscuits if you stretch to those.

Stephen   No, I'm afraid we don't. They're more of a 'trattoria' sort of thing I think you'll find. There's a reasonable one nearby I can recommend . . . if you're desperate.

Ash   I'm OK here, thanks.

Stephen   So you are. Good night.

Stephen *exits into kitchen.*

Kitchen.

Stephen   Come on, Mugsy.

Mugsy (*off*)   I am coming on.

Stephen   Pour me a glass of that, Frankie.

Frankie *pours.*

Frankie   What's he doing in there?

Stephen   I think he's being snide about my restaurant.

Frankie   Must be from *The Good Food Guide*.

Sweeney   He weren't having a pop at my cooking, was he?

Stephen   No, he was having a 'pop' at me actually.

He drinks.

What's this?

Frankie   Wine.

Stephen   This is good claret.

Frankie   Table Four sent it back.

Stephen   Table Four were drinking mineral water all night.

Beat.

Frankie   That's why they sent it back.

Stephen   Show me the bottle. Frankie, show me the bottle.

Frankie *shows him the label.*

Stephen   Frankie, the next time you want to steal a forty-pound bottle of wine you could at least have the decency to ask.

Frankie   Isn't that a contradiction in terms?

Stephen   Don't fuck around with me Frankie, this is theft.

Mugsy *enters with the cafetière.*

Frankie   I'll pay for it.

Stephen   You bet you will.

Frankie   Trade price by the way, no mark-up.

Stephen   You'll pay forty pounds for it.

Frankie *puts the other bottle on the table.*

Frankie   Eighty. Tell you what, why don't you knock it off my winnings tonight?

Stephen   It's not funny, Frankie.

Frankie   I'm not laughing.

Stephen   Neither am I.

Frankie   Well, I think we've established it's not funny then.

Stephen *rises.*

Sweeney   Girls, girls, girls. I told him he could have it, Stephen, take it out my wages.

Stephen   It's a touching gesture, Sweeney, but you're a pathetic liar. (*To* **Mugsy**.) GET A MOVE ON.

Stephen *exits.* **Mugsy** *exits into restaurant.* **Frankie** *takes out a pack of cigarettes.* **Sweeney** *takes them from him.*

Sweeney   Come on.

Frankie *and* **Sweeney** *exit.*

Restaurant.

Mugsy *places the cafetière on* **Ash**'s *table.*

Mugsy   One cafetière. Just give it a couple of minutes and then you press this thing down, quite slowly so it doesn't all . . . ruffle up . . . and then . . . well, that's it.

Ash   Cheers.

Mugsy   And I'm afraid we don't have any of those . . . biscuits.

Ash   No problem.

Mugsy   I've got a Snickers if you want.

Beat.

Ash   OK.

Mugsy   What?

Ash   I said OK. I'll have it.

Pause.

Mugsy   Right. I thought you'd say no.

Ash   Have you got one or not?

Mugsy   Yeah . . . but I've eaten half of it.

Beat.

Ash   Well, I'll have the other half.

Mugsy   Right, I'll just go and get it.

Ash   Sliced.

Mugsy   What?

Ash   I want it sliced . . . on a little side-plate.

Mugsy   Right.

Mugsy *exits into kitchen and off.* **Ash** *takes out his mobile phone and makes a call.*

Ash   Hallo . . . yeah . . . I've been held up . . . half an hour . . . yes, I'll be there.

Mugsy *returns with a side-plate.*

Mugsy   One Snickers, sliced, on a little side-plate.

Ash   Thanks.

Ash *presses down the cafetière.*

Mugsy   SLOWLY.

Ash *looks at him.*

Mugsy   Slowly. Is there anything else?

Ash   Why, am I keeping you up?

Mugsy   No, it's just that . . . we've got a bit of a poker game starting downstairs and we can't start until –

Ash   Until I've pissed off.

Mugsy   No, no, you stay as long as you like. Really, I've got all night to take their money.

Beat.

So . . . shall I get the bill then?

Ash   Why, you paying?

Mugsy   No. Oh, you paying, very good. No, no I'm not. So shall I get the bill?

Pause.

Ash   Carl's paying.

Mugsy   Carl?

Ash   Yeah.

Mugsy   So you know Carl then?

Ash   Yeah, he's late.

Mugsy   Yeah, he's always late. How d'you know him?

Ash   I'm his father.

Pause.

Mugsy   But . . .

Ash   Don't be daft. Quiet tonight here, how's this place doing?

Mugsy *goes to the bar and begins to prepare the bill.*

Mugsy OK, could be better. It's the management really . . . and the location . . . and the food. It needs . . . vision.

Ash So what are you playing tonight?

Mugsy Poker.

Ash I know, you said, I meant what stakes?

Mugsy Depends, starts small gets big, depends who's doing 'em. I always say it's no fun unless it hurts.

Ash You play with more than you can afford?

Mugsy Yeah.

Ash What's the ante?

Mugsy Two from the dealer.

Ash Live blind?

Mugsy Uh huh.

Ash Dealer's Choice?

Mugsy Yep.

Ash Pot limit?

Mugsy It starts pot limit and then about four in the morning the losers demand no limit.

Ash You play with wilds?

Mugsy You bet we do.

Ash So what's your game?

Mugsy You name it; Hold'em, Omaha, Irish, Lowball, Fiery Cross, Anaconda – I won't charge you for the Snickers.

Ash You're spoiling me.

Mugsy Chicago, Hedgehog, Mugsy's Nightmare –

Ash What's that?

Mugsy Mugsy's Nightmare? I invented that one; it's five-card stud, hi-lo, two down, three up, whores, fours and one-eyed jacks wild with a twist. The twist being I'm the only one who understands it.

Ash   Cards speak or declarations?

Mugsy   Either, it's dealer's choice.

Ash   Flushes count hi-lo?

Mugsy   Yep.

Ash   The wheel goes?

Mugsy   Everything goes. So you're a poker player then?

Ash   Me? No.

Carl *enters*.

Carl   Hi, Ash.

Ash   Hi, Carl.

Mugsy   Carl, Carl, how did it go?

Carl   What?

Mugsy   With Stephen. The restaurant.

Carl   Went well, Mugsy.

Mugsy   Yes. I'm about to see him to –

Carl   Hi, Ash, sorry I'm late.

Ash   No problem.

Carl   Good meal?

Ash   Terrific. Thank you.

Mugsy   The bill. Carl? This gentleman said you –

Carl   Yeah.

He gets his wallet out.

This is the famous Mugsy. Has he been serving you?

Ash   Yeah, very well, thank you.

Mugsy   Cheers. Twenty-nine pounds fifty, Carl.

Carl *gives* **Mugsy** *thirty pounds*.

Mugsy   Service?

Carl *gives him five pounds*.

Thank you, please come again.

Beat.

Do you want some more coffee?

Ash   No.

Mugsy   I'll . . . I'll go in here then.

Ash   Right.

Mugsy *exits into kitchen and off.*

Pause.

Carl   So how's it going?

Ash   Yeah, OK.

Pause.

Carl   Did you meet my father?

Ash   Yeah.

Carl   As I said? Anal or what?

Ash   He's OK.

Carl   Yeah, he's OK.

Pause.

Ash   Where is it?

Carl   I haven't got it . . . not all of it.

Ash   How much have you got?

Carl   Two hundred and sixty-five.

Pause.

Ash   You owe me four grand.

Beat.

Where is it?

Carl   It's . . . gone.

Ash   What do you mean it's 'gone'?

Carl   Casino, I've just been. I lost it. I mean I had a grand, really, I tried to win the other three playing blackjack, the dealer was on a freak roll. I was playing hundred quid a box . . . I was trying to count – like you taught me . . . he was hitting aces and tens non-stop. Ash, I'm sorry.

Beat.

Are you going to kill me?

Ash   Jesus, he thinks he's in a movie.

Beat.

I told you it had to be tonight.

Carl   I know.

Ash   I've been telling you for three months you had to pay it tonight.

Carl   I know.

Ash   I owe this money.

Carl   I know.

Ash   I have to go to a game now and pay this money.

Carl   I know.

Beat.

Ash   All right, fine. You said you could always get it off your father. Go and get it off your father.

Carl   I'm sorry, I can't.

Ash   Listen fuckbrain, you go to your nice father now and you tell him what a sad sorry little prick you are for spunking all this money and you tell him the truth and you promise him you'll never gamble again because you're a fucking loser and you get me my money. Now.

Carl   And what if I can't?

Ash (*sarcastic*)   They'll come in here with big guns and blow your brains out. BANG.

*He hits **Carl**, once. Hard.*

You fucking idiot. It's serious. It's a poker debt. It has to be paid. You said, you said when I lent you this, this year, all this year, you said your father was a soft touch, your father the rich businessman with his swank fucking restaurant. You said he'd give you the money if it came to it. Well, this is it. Go get the money, go crying, go begging, go suck his fucking cock I don't care, just get the fucking money.

Beat.

You want me to go in there and get it?

Carl   No, he doesn't know about the gambling. He thinks I've stopped. I can't . . . it would kill him, he'd kill me. Ash, I do love him, he's my father.

Ash   You think I care?

Carl   Yes. Come on . . . you like me.

Ash   Like is irrelevant.

Carl   Please . . .

Ash   Can't do it, Carl. This is fucked up. Get the money.

Carl   Please don't make me.

Ash   Right, I'll do it.

Carl   No, no, listen, why don't you play tonight? In our game, here, you'll clean up.

Ash   Clean up? In a baby's game. What do I win? A packet of Smarties.

Carl   There's money here, there's money I promise. They're all shit. Mugsy lost three grand a month ago. Sometimes the game goes mental, everyone goes on tilt –

Ash   You think there's four grand here?

Carl   Maybe not four, three maybe –

Ash   I need four.

Carl   There's four, there's four. How much do you owe?

Ash   Ten.

Beat.

Carl   How much have you got?

Ash   Five, plus your fucking 'four'.

Carl (*close*)   Please. Come on . . . you're a professional . . .
it's easy money . . .

Silence.

Ash   Who's playing?

Carl   Me, Mugsy, Sweeney – plays like a madman, can't
pass, pure aggression, no brains. Dad, granite . . . just push
the right buttons he's easy. And Frankie, he's quite good.

Ash   What does that mean?

Carl   He's a bit flash, likes to mix it up.

Ash   And he's quite good?

Carl   In this game, yeah. But you'll kill him. Please. Help.

Pause. **Ash** *looks at* **Carl**. *Close.* **Ash** *takes out his mobile phone. He
exits.* **Carl** *is left alone in the restaurant.*

Kitchen.

Enter **Sweeney** *and* **Frankie**. **Sweeney** *holding an airline ticket.*

Sweeney   So where you going?

Sweeney *reads the ticket, stunned.*

Frankie (*taking the ticket*)   Las Vegas, mate, the States. The
US of A.

Sweeney   When?

Frankie   It's an open ticket, soon as I've saved enough
money, couple of months.

Sweeney   To do what?

Frankie   Play poker . . .

Sweeney   You? Turn professional poker player?

Frankie   Yeah . . . why not?

Pause.

Sweeney Because . . . but it doesn't mean you have to . . . what about . . . everything here?

Frankie What 'here'?

Sweeney Here . . . I dunno, me . . . Mugsy . . .

Frankie You can come and visit me in my five-star suite at Caesar's Palace. I'll lay on some broads.

Pause.

Sweeney I shouldn't play tonight.

Frankie You said you'd play . . . I mean . . . don't play if you don't want to.

Sweeney I don't want to let the boys down.

Frankie Play for a while, see how it goes.

Sweeney You want my money?

Frankie No . . . Yeah.

Pause.

Sweeney So how much you got saved, Frank?

Frankie A few grand. One big win and I'm sorted. I'm going, Sween, there's no way I'm not going. I've got the ticket, Sween, one way. Business class. I've been saying for years I'm going to leave this shithole.

Sweeney What shithole?

Frankie This place, London, England, everywhere. This country's a shanty town. It's dead, Sween.

Sweeney So go to Vegas.

Restaurant.

Ash *enters.*

Ash You're lucky.

Carl Thanks.

Ash Three hours and that's it, I go to your father.

Carl Thank you.

Ash   Why d'you piss me about?

Carl   I haven't done it on purpose.

Ash   What about all the meals at the casino? The money? The drinks, the late nights, the cabs. I've given you my time. I taught you how to play. I've covered your debts for a year. I trusted you . . . and you repay me like . . . you're compulsive.

Carl   And you're not?

Ash   No, only thing I'm addicted to is these. (*He holds up his cigarette.*)

Carl   Sorry, can I have one?

Ash   Fuck off. Get your own.

Carl   Come on, don't be like my dad.

Ash   I'm not like your dad, Carl – I don't care about you.

Pause.

Carl   I . . . thought you liked me?

Beat.

Ash   Not especially.

Pause.

Carl   Why do you . . . why did you let me play in your game?

Ash   The big boys' game?

Carl   Yes.

Ash   Cos you're a mug. You're value.

Pause.

Carl   So . . . if you don't like me, why don't you go to him now and get the money . . . what is this?

Ash   Pity.

Carl   You pity me?

Ash   No, your father.

Silence.

Carl   Who shall I say you are?

Ash   What do you mean?

Carl   I can't say this is Ash, he's a professional poker player, is it OK if he sits down and takes your money.

Ash   Say what you like, it's your problem.

Carl   You're my teacher, ex-teacher.

Ash   From where?

Carl   School.

Ash   What a fucking mess.

Kitchen.

Enter **Mugsy**.

Mugsy   Seen Stephen?

Frankie   No.

Mugsy *exits into*

Restaurant.

Mugsy   Seen your dad?

Carl   No.

Mugsy (*to* **Ash**)   Sorry, everything OK?

Ash   Fine.

Carl   Mugs, do you reckon it'd be OK if Ash sat in with us tonight?

Mugsy   Dunno, better ask your dad. I thought you didn't play?

Ash   I play a bit, I'm learning.

Mugsy   Yeah, got to start somewhere. We'll teach you. (*To* **Carl**.) He must be downstairs setting up. Will you tell him I want words.

Carl   Yeah.

Mugsy Mile End!

Carl (*to* **Ash**) OK?

Ash Smashing.

Carl Mugs, when you're talking to dad, don't mention the figures, talk generally. We've got to deal with him carefully, OK?

Mugsy I think I know how to handle a business situation.

Carl Just don't talk about the actual sums involved.

Mugsy The grand?

Carl Exactly. We might want more, start up capital, let's be flexible, eh?

Mugsy Flexible, like it.

Carl *exits into*

Kitchen.

Sweeney You got my money, Carl?

Carl No.

Carl *exits.*

Sweeney Here, Frankie, do us a favour, look after this?

Frankie What . . .

He hands **Frankie** *some cash.*

Sweeney Fifty quid. Don't let me touch it.

Frankie OK.

Sweeney I'm serious. Don't let me play with it.

Frankie OK.

Restaurant.

Mugsy So where did you say you knew Carl from?

Ash I didn't say. I used to . . .

Mugsy What?

Ash No, nothing.

Mugsy   You were saying? You used to . . .

Ash   I used to be his teacher.

Mugsy   Oh right, what subject?

Beat.

Ash   Economics.

Mugsy   Economics, always useful. Money makes the world go round and all that. Here, you know in medieval times when they didn't know the earth was round, do you reckon they said 'Money makes the world go flat'?

Ash   Yeah, probably.

Mugsy   So where did you teach Carl? He went to some boarding school, didn't he?

Ash   Yeah.

Mugsy   Personally I think it's cruel, packing your kids off to some place in the country full of poofs, no offence.

Ash   I don't teach any more.

Mugsy   Oh right, what d'you do now? I see you've got the old mobile there, you in business?

Ash   Yeah.

Mugsy   What sort?

Ash   Investment.

Mugsy   Right. What exactly is investment? I mean, I know what investment is but what . . . what is it exactly?

Ash   Give it a fucking rest, will you.

Beat.

Mugsy   Sorry. I do go on a bit sometimes.

Mugsy *exits into*

Kitchen.

Mugsy   I don't believe it, I see it but I don't believe it.

Frankie   Caught your own reflection?

Mugsy   Carl just invited that bloke to play tonight.

Frankie   You what?

Mugsy   Serious. I've been sussing him out.

Frankie   Ooo, Sherlock Mugsy.

Mugsy   Listen, I've learnt all about him thus giving me the edge over you mugs.

Sweeney   So what's he like, Miss Marple?

Mugsy   Seems all right, bit weird.

Frankie   Is he rich?

Mugsy   Yeah, he's an investor.

Frankie   In what?

Mugsy   I dunno.

Frankie   What does he look like?

Mugsy   Like a bloke.

Frankie   Does he look like a mug?

Mugsy   I don't know.

Sweeney   Using your powers of psychological nuance would you say he looks like a mug?

Mugsy   I don't know, what does a mug look like?

Sweeney and **Frankie** *laugh.*

Frankie (*to* **Sweeney**)   That means you don't have to play . . .

Sweeney   I'll play, I'm all right.

Mugsy   You wait till tonight. I shall roast you. I shall have your scrotums on a silver platter.

Frankie   Delicacy of 'Mugsy's Mile End Bistro Shithouse'?

Mugsy   Yes very witty. You won't be laughing when I slip your flattened bollocks into my wallet.

Frankie   What, like you did four weeks ago?

Sweeney Was that on a certain night?

Frankie What night would that be?

Mugsy Oi.

Sweeney I forget, was it?

Frankie Was it . . . no it couldn't have been –

Sweeney I think it was . . .

Mugsy Stop mentioning it, no one mentions the unmentionable.

Frankie What? The unmentionable night you lost three grand to our beloved employer?

Mugsy He should never've been in that hand. It was the outdraw of the century –

Sweeney Tell us about it, Mugs.

Frankie For a change.

Mugsy It's Hold'em. I've got aces, right. It's my button, I raise before the flop, everyone passes, Stephen back-raises me, I think right, I'll slow-play from now on.

Frankie Maestro.

Mugsy What does it flop? Only queen, queen, ace, I've only flopped a house, I've only flopped the stone bonking unbeatable rock of Gibraltar Bank of England nuts.

Sweeney *and* **Frankie** Yes.

Mugsy The Turn, no help, I check.

Sweeney Genius.

Mugsy Last card, what comes? The only card I don't want to see, the only card that beats me.

Sweeney A queen.

Frankie That's when you should've passed.

Mugsy I didn't know he'd made four queens.

Frankie It was obvious, he bet a grand at you. Play the man not the cards. You fell in love with your hand.

Mugsy   Wouldn't you?

Frankie   You were unlucky.

Mugsy   Unlucky? Have you any idea what the odds are for him hitting a queen on the last card?

Frankie   Forty-three to one against.

Beat.

Mugsy   Er . . . yeah, exactly, forty-three to one against.

Sweeney   You were unlucky, Mugs, how many more times do you want to hear it?

Mugsy   Do you realise how many hours overtime I'm doing to pay off that debt? I haven't had a day off in three weeks, I'm working every Saturday night and I had to cancel my holiday, I was going to take my mum to Disneyland. I'd saved up specially.

Frankie   You still shouldn't have called on the end.

Mugsy   How can you pass aces?

Frankie   Sometimes you have to.

Mugsy   I know. I knew I'd lost but I still called. Why? Why did I call?

Frankie   Because you are a mug, Mugs.

Mugsy   It was so unfair.

Frankie   You expect justice at a poker table?

Mugsy   I'll win it back tonight, you'll see.

Sweeney   Win back three grand? You've got more chance of teaching a rocking horse to shit.

Mugsy   Where is he anyway, we're supposed to be discussing business.

Frankie   Probably ironing the baize. No crinkles on the baize –

Sweeney   No crinkles on the baize.

Mugsy   No crinkles on the baize.

Frankie   Fucking nutter.

Stephen *enters.*

Stephen   My children. The game is on. The Poker Room awaits.

Mugsy   At long last, it's like waiting for King Canute.

Pause.

Stephen   In what possible sense is it like waiting for King Canute?

Pause.

Frankie (*under his breath*)   King Cunt.

Pause. **Stephen** *smiles.*

Stephen   Downstairs, scum.

Frankie *and* **Sweeney** *exit.*

Mugsy   Right, Stephen, can we get down to business please?

Stephen   Just a moment, Mugs.

Stephen *enters*

Restaurant.

Stephen   My son tells me you'd like to play with us tonight.

Ash   Yeah, if that's all right with you.

Stephen   I look forward to it.

Beat. They look at each other.

Your waiter will bring you down in a minute.

Stephen *exits into*

Kitchen.

Mugsy   Right, Stephen, business. Now, the key to this scheme is . . . flexibility. I see you as a man of vision and I see your role in this scheme as that of a silent partner, who can speak, but in a quiet advisory capacity . . . are you all right?

Stephen Look, Mugs, I have to tell you that I think my son is the last person in the world that anyone ought to go into business with.

Mugsy You've got a very fair point.

Stephen Mugsy, I don't want to disappoint you but –

Mugsy It's all right, I've anticipated your concerns; you're worried I'll steal your trade. A reasonable anxiety for a proprietor. I'm prepared to offer you a deal, Stephen . . . we open on alternate nights.

Stephen Mugsy, that's not it –

Mugsy It's the staff? You're worried I'll take Sweeney and Frankie with me. Once again, that is reasonable, now I can offer you a job-share scheme whereby –

Stephen No Mugs –

Mugsy Is it because of the location?

Stephen Of course not.

Mugsy Is it because it's a toilet?

Stephen I'm sorry?

Mugsy Is it because the proposed property is at present a public convenience because once you've seen it you'll –

Stephen *bursts out laughing.*

Mugsy What?

Stephen I'm sorry, Mugs.

He laughs again.

Mugsy Didn't Carl tell you?

Stephen No, he most certainly did not. No, he edited that tiny piece of information right out of the scheme, Mugsy. I wonder why?

Stephen *laughs again.*

Mugsy What exactly is the joke?

Stephen　You want to open a restaurant in a toilet with my son – that'll do for me.

Mugsy　I thought you were a man of vision.

Stephen　I've got the vision to see it lends a whole new meaning to the term 'convenience food'.

Mugsy　Very funny, I've heard all the jokes.

Stephen　Good evening, sir, your usual cubicle?

Mugsy　Why can't you just think about the idea, for one second without immediately –

Stephen　All right, I'm sorry, Mugs.

Mugsy　I'm not a mug, you know, I'm not in actual fact a mug.

Stephen　OK, I'm sorry.

Beat.

OK, seriously . . . don't you think it might be a problem with the ladies and gents having to dine separately?

He laughs again.

Mugsy　Will you fucking take me seriously. It can change, it's not going to be a toilet. What was this place before you bought it?

Stephen　A butcher's.

Mugsy　A butcher's, right, well, I don't see people coming in here saying 'I want to buy a pound of sausages'. People aren't going to come into my restaurant and have a crap on the dining-room floor. It's gonna change.

Stephen　Point taken.

Mugsy　You're treating me disrespectfully, Stephen, you can't push me about just cos you're in charge, I'm not your fucking son.

Stephen　What's that supposed to mean?

Mugsy   It's not difficult to run a restaurant I'll tell you that.

Stephen   Listen, Mugs, listen. I'm sorry for laughing, really. Look, we get on well you and I, we have good rapport, you're a much valued member of my staff.

Mugsy   Yeah, well.

Stephen   Yeah well what? It's true, you've been here since day one, the customers are very fond of you, you're indispensable.

Mugsy   You think I'm a good waiter?

Stephen   You're my top man, you're my head waiter.

Mugsy   What does that mean? You don't pay me more than anyone else, I'm working night and day for you, I'm working my balls off.

Stephen   You know why that is. Mugs, you're like family – better than family, we actually get on.

Mugsy   Exactly, so you don't want to lose me so you won't help me in my business, that's what's going on underneath. You can't see it cos it's buried so deep but I know you Stephen, I can read you, that's what I think.

Stephen   All right, that's what you think.

Mugsy   You want to hold me back.

Stephen   All right. You can choose to take this however you want but I think it's the truth. I think you're angry because you're paying off a poker debt in the only way you can which is by working overtime, by working your balls off –

Mugsy   No –

Stephen   Just let me finish please, and you find it humiliating – but there is no other way, I can't just scrub the debt.

Mugsy   You outdrew me.

Stephen   Yes I did, I'm sorry, it was bad luck. Nothing more nothing less.

Mugsy   Yeah, but I'm the only one suffering for it.

Stephen   You lost, Mugsy, losing hurts.

Pause.

And this restaurant you want to open . . . it's not *real* Mugs . . . opening a restaurant is a huge risk, nine out of ten don't survive. You know nothing about this business; dealing with suppliers, tax returns, employment law –

Mugsy   I could learn, you did.

Stephen   You could but it's hard.

Mugsy   I could do it.

Stephen   I'm not saying you couldn't.

Mugsy   You think it, you think I couldn't.

Stephen   I think . . . that you're good at the job that you do. I also think that you don't, in your heart, really *want* to open a restaurant. I think it scares you. And I think you're disappointed with yourself that it scares you. Believe me, Mugs, I do understand disappointment.

Pause.

Mugsy   That's what you think is it?

Stephen   That's what I think.

Beat.

Mugsy   I've got to . . .

Stephen   OK?

Mugsy   Yeah, OK.

Stephen   I'm going downstairs. OK.

Mugsy   YES OK.

Stephen *turns at exit.*

Stephen   Mugsy . . . will you bring him down for me please?

Mugsy   Yeah.

Stephen *exits.* **Mugsy** *sits alone in the kitchen. He takes his shirt off and puts on a bright Hawaiian shirt from his bag and also the new tie he was wearing earlier.*

Enter **Frankie**.

Frankie   So?

Mugsy   He's interested . . . he's definitely interested. He's having a think about it but he's interested.

Frankie   Great.

Beat.

You coming down?

Mugsy   Yeah. Am I a mug?

Frankie   Course you're not.

He takes the pack of cards from the kitchen table.

Come on, we're starting.

Mugsy   Yeah.

Frankie *exits.* **Mugsy** *exits into*

Restaurant.

Mugsy   We're starting.

Ash   Right. Nice shirt.

Mugsy   Thanks . . . lucky poker shirt.

He leads **Ash** *out of the restaurant and through the kitchen.*

It's this way . . .

He stops at the exit.

You say you're in the investment business?

Ash (*off*)   Yeah.

Mugsy   Do you know the Mile End Road?

Act Three

Scene One

Basement.

Late night.

The atmosphere of this room should be noticeably different from the sleek environments of Acts One and Two. A battered fridge, **Stephen***'s desk with a computer on it and a framed photo of* **Carl***, aged five, filing cabinets, empty crates etc.*

The game is in progress. The players are seated at a table covered with a green baize cloth. **Ash** *at one o'clock,* **Carl** *at three,* **Sweeney** *five,* **Frankie** *seven,* **Mugsy** *nine and* **Stephen** *at eleven.* **Ash** *has just dealt. They are playing 'Omaha'. Each player has four cards in his hand. This is the first round of betting.*

Carl   Call. (*He puts in two pounds in chips.*)

Sweeney   Okey Dokey. (*Likewise.*)

Frankie   Call. (*Etc.*)

Mugsy   I call.

Stephen   Yup.

Ash   Raise ten.

Carl   No. (*He passes his cards into the middle.*)

Sweeney   Yep.

Frankie   Call.

Mugsy   Calling for the value.

Frankie   You tilty bastard.

Mugsy   I'm not on tilt.

Frankie   You're horizontal.

Mugsy   Just for that I shall re-raise, the bet is Tony's pregnant sister.

Stephen   What?

Mugsy   Fifteen, mate.

Laughter.

Stephen (*referring to the tie*)   I thought I told you to remove that monstrosity.

Mugsy   Your dictatorship ended two hours ago. Poker law has been declared. The tie stays. Your bet, Stevie boy.

Stephen   Don't call me that. Pass.

Mugsy *makes chicken noises*.

Mugsy   Go on, Stevie boy, have a flutter for once in your life, you granite bastard.

Stephen   It's poker, Mugsy, not the bloody lottery.

Mugsy   Poker without gambling is like sex without orgasm.

Frankie   What would you know? Last time Mugsy had an orgasm you know what came out . . . dust.

Mugsy   Losing tonight are you by any chance, Francis?

Frankie   Switch off.

Stephen   Gentlemen, we have a guest.

Ash   Fifteen, call.

Sweeney   Yep.

Frankie   Call. Flop 'em.

Ash *deals the flop, i.e. he turns over three 'communal' cards face up on the table*.

Ash   Jack of spades, seven of spades, ten of diamonds.

Mugsy   Deemonds! (*A refrain he shouts whenever a diamond is dealt*.)

Sweeney   Fifty quid.

Frankie   Call.

Mugsy Oh, my good friend, Sweeney Ted, I'm afraid I'm going to have to raise your arse. There's your fifty and I raise one hundred pounds sterling.

Sweeney Want a caller, Mugs?

Mugsy Two preferably.

Frankie Reckon your straight's gonna stand up?

Mugsy More than your trips are, loser.

Ash I raise . . . three hundred.

Laughter.

Sweeney Pass.

Frankie Pass. Bye bye, Mugsy.

Mugsy Three hundred?

Frankie Three hundred.

Mugsy Three hundred?

Ash Three hundred.

Sweeney THREE HUNDRED.

Carl Pass, Mugsy.

Frankie What a poker face.

Mugsy Shut up, I'm thinking.

Sweeney We can see that, we can see your brain sweating, it's dribbling out your arse'ole, mate.

Mugsy Shut up. Who raised before the flop?

All You.

Laughter.

Mugsy He must have the eight nine of spades. I can't call.

Stephen Is that a pass, Mugs?

Mugsy No.

Stephen Come on, it's not chess.

Mugsy Yeah, well, you obviously haven't read Herbert O. Yardley, 'Poker is chess with money'.

Stephen Not the way you play it.

Mugsy What day is it?

Sweeney Oh, for fuck's sake, Sunday.

Stephen Monday actually.

Mugsy No, I meant what date.

Carl The ninth.

Mugsy Odd number, right . . . no, hold on . . . How much is in the pot?

Carl About five hundred.

Frankie Here Mugs, that's half a toilet.

Laughter.

Stephen Actually, Frankie, it's one sixth of a toilet. You never were very good at maths –

Carl Pass, Mugsy.

Sweeney Come on, you mug, I'm growing a beard here.

Mugsy Shut up, it's a big pot, PLEASE. Eight nine of spades. He's got eight nine of spades . . . I'd stake my reputation on it.

Ash I'd prefer your money.

Pause.

Mugsy Call.

Stephen The bet is called.

Mugsy He's bluffing.

Frankie Bollocks.

Ash OK?

Mugsy Oh yes.

Ash *deals another card face up.*

Ash   Four of diamonds.

Mugsy   Deemonds.

Ash   Your bet.

Mugsy   One hundred and forty-six all in.

Ash   Call.

Mugsy   Shit.

Frankie   He's got eight nine of spades.

Mugsy   That's where you're wrong, the reason why I called is that I had a hunch he had eight nine of spades but I distrusted my hunch because I've had a cold recently.

Stephen   Come on, on their backs.

Mugsy *and* **Ash** *turn their cards over. Laughter.*

Mugsy   I don't believe it, I do not believe it. Eight nine of spades. (*To* **Ash**.) Don't turn a spade over, don't turn a spade over. No spade, no spade, DON'T TURN A FUCKING SPADE OVER. I can't look . . . Frankie, tell me what comes.

Mugsy *turns away.* **Ash** *turns a card over.*

Frankie   Ten of spades . . . tough luck, Mugs.

Mugsy   Fuck, fuck, fuck, fuck, fuck, fuck, fuck, fuck.

Frankie   Sorry, my mistake, ten of clubs, split pot.

Mugsy (*relieved*)   You cunt.

Laughter.

Frankie   Trick of the light, mate.

Stephen   Come on, split it up. Half each.

Mugsy   Jesus, my whole life just flashed before my eyes.

Frankie   Any good?

Mugsy   No, you were in it.

Stephen   Next case.

Mugsy (*to* **Ash**)   Sorry, mate, I lost my cool there for a second.

Laughter.

Ash   I think I've got a full house.

Laughter stops.

Stephen   Where?

Ash   There, it paired the board. Tens on Jacks.

Carl   He's right . . .

Ash   Sorry, mate.

Ash *rakes in the chips.*

Mugsy   Shit, I didn't see it. Fuck shit tit piss wank fuck bollocks.

Stephen   Bad luck, Mugs.

Mugsy   I've just done five hundred quid.

Frankie   The night is young.

Mugsy   Carl, you might have warned us – he's got the lot.

Ash   Beginner's luck.

Stephen   Again. Your deal, Carl.

Carl   Any requests?

Mugsy   Yeah, I'd like to win please.

Sweeney   He said requests not miracles.

Mugsy   You winning then, Sween?

Sweeney   No one's winning except him.

Carl   Five-card draw, jacks or better.

Scene Two

Later.

Sweeney (*singing to the tune of 'I Could've Danced All Night'*)   I haven't seen a card all night, I haven't seen a card all night. I haven't seen a card all night. Right, everyone, if I lose this lot I'm going.

Mugsy   Bye, mate. The Hospital for Poker Casualties is just along the road.

Stephen   Mugsy will show you the way.

Sweeney   One last shot.

Mugsy   And the game is Mugsy's Nightmare.

Stephen   Deal me out.

Mugsy (*to* **Ash**)   Stephen doesn't like Mugsy's Nightmare.

Stephen   I like playing poker not bloody roulette.

Frankie   You don't like playing poker, Stephen. You like winning.

Stephen   Thank you, Sigmund. Come on, Mugsy, choose a grown-up game.

Mugsy   It's Dealer's Choice. I'm the dealer I'll play what I want.

Sweeney   Just deal.

Mugsy *begins to deal two cards to each player.*

Mugsy   Out?

Stephen   Yes, OUT.

Mugsy   Ooo.

Sweeney   Will someone remind me of the rules of this ridiculous fucking game . . .

Mugsy   Five-card stud, hi-lo, two down, three up, whores, fours and one-eyed jacks wild, cards speak, eight or better for the low, the wheel goes, suicide king up you lose automatically.

Stephen   It's not poker, it's bloody bingo for brain surgeons. The game is like its inventor – a freak mutation.

Mugsy   So don't play, Lemon.

Stephen   I'm not playing, Toilet.

Mugsy   Ash?

Ash   Pass.

Stephen   Very wise.

Carl   Call two.

Mugsy   Good boy.

Sweeney   I call.

Frankie (*reluctant*)   Go on then.

Mugsy   No raise from the dealer.

He deals an up card to **Carl**, **Sweeney**, **Frankie** *and himself.*

Three of clubs, jack of clubs, two-eyed, six of deemonds and ten of deemonds. Double deemonds. Jack to speak.

Sweeney   Eight.

Frankie   Yeah.

Mugsy   One fat lezza going in.

Sweeney   What?

Mugsy   Eight.

Sweeney   Well, say it.

Mugsy   Ooo.

Carl   Call eight.

Mugsy *deals another up card to* **Carl**, **Sweeney**, **Frankie** *and himself.*

Mugsy   Nine of hearts busted low, five of clubs possible flush, seven of spades straightening, queen of hearts wild. Tens are on the potty. What is it?

Frankie   Forty.

Mugsy   Mid-life crisis, forty.

Carl   Pass.

Sweeney   Call.

Frankie   Yep. How old are you, Stephen?

Stephen   I can't remember.

Frankie   Enjoying your mid-life crisis?

Stephen   Yes, it began when you started working here.

Sweeney   Can we play cards please?

Mugsy   We can, dunno about you.

He deals an up card to **Sweeney**.

Eight of clubs, still possible . . .

And then **Frankie**.

King of hearts . . . bad luck, mate.

Frankie   What d'you mean?

Mugsy   Suicide king you lose automatically.

Frankie   You what?

Mugsy   Bye bye.

Frankie   You never said.

All   Yes he did.

Beat.

Frankie   What a stupid poxy little game.

Stephen   You were warned.

Frankie   WHAT A FEEBLE FUCKING FARCE.

Sweeney   Could you please SHUT UP.

Mugsy   Shh, shh, everyone quiet for Sween, he's doing his bollocks, quiet.

Sweeney   Deal, Mugs.

Mugsy (*deals a final up card to himself*)   Four of hearts. Check.

Pause.

Sweeney (*to* **Frankie**)   You got that fifty?

Pause.

Frank . . . the fifty.

Frankie *gives* **Sweeney** *fifty pounds in cash.*

Sweeney Let's see what you're made of, Mugsy. There's fifty plus forty . . . seven . . . that's ninety seven all in.

Mugsy Call.

Sweeney What you got, Mugs?

Mugsy Five tens.

Pause.

Sweeney How the fuck can you have 'five tens', there's only four in the pack and I've got one of them.

Mugsy I've got queen four in the box, my son, four wilds.

Mugsy *turns over his cards.*

Beat.

Sweeney You win.

Mugsy Yes! I wish you'd had more money, Sween, you'd have done your bollocks, roasted like a kipper, mate. It's my night, I told you, Mugsy's back, the Mug is back.

Frankie You winning then?

Mugsy No, but I'm on the way. What d'you have, Sween?

Sweeney Flush.

Frankie You can't call with that.

Sweeney I just did.

Frankie And you lost.

Sweeney Yeah, all right.

Frankie Just trying to help.

Sweeney You winning?

Frankie No but –

Sweeney Well, then, stop being such an expert Mr Vegas.

Stephen Lovers' tiff all over now, is it? Your deal, Frankie.

Sweeney *gets up.*

Sweeney I'm out of here.

Frankie Seven stud hi-lo.

Sweeney Can I grab a beer, Stephen?

Stephen Yup.

Sweeney *goes to the fridge but decides against taking a beer.*
Frankie *starts to deal.*

Sweeney (*sings*) I haven't seen a card all night, I haven't seen a card all night. I haven't seen a card all night, I –

Stephen Sweeney.

Sweeney Good evening?

Stephen There's a game on . . .

Sweeney Sorry, sorry.

Frankie (*to* **Mugsy**) Your bet.

Sweeney I haven't seen a card all night, I haven't seen a card all night, I haven't seen a card all night –

Stephen Sweeney.

Sweeney Your Highness?

Stephen You know the house rules, Sweeney, if you're not in the game you're not in the room.

Sweeney Sorry, I forgot.

Frankie Mugs, you to bet.

Sweeney I HAVEN'T SEEN A CARD ALL NIGHT, I HAVEN'T SEEN A CARD ALL NIGHT, I HAVEN'T SEEN A CARD ALL FUCKING NIGHT –

Stephen If you're not in the game you're not in the room. House Rules.

Sweeney What does it matter, Stephen, what the fuck does it matter?

Stephen It matters, Sweeney, because rules are rules.

Sweeney They're *your* rules, Stephen, no one else gives a flying fuck. 'No smoking' – have you ever heard anything so ridiculous for a poker school? No beers on the table unless they're on these poxy little beer mats. Oi . . . Ash, see this baize, this tatty bit of shit, he takes it home every Sunday night, religiously, and irons it, he fucking irons it, the c –

He is now close to tears.

He's got a computer, what does he keep on it? Accounts? Invoices? No, he keeps a record of all the games we've played, with lots of little coloured graphs and charts. He lives for his poker. He can tell you who won the game and with what hand on Easter Sunday six fucking years ago.

Stephen Yuh I can, you lost. You chose to play tonight, Sweeney, don't use your self-hatred as a weapon against us.

Sweeney Stephen, you are such a wanker, you are such an unbelievable fucking wanker.

Stephen Good night.

Sweeney What is your fucking problem?

Stephen I don't think I have a problem. I just want to play a quiet game of cards on a Sunday night without you in the background sloshing around in a sea of self-pity. Call.

Ash Call.

Carl Call.

Sweeney Come on, Frankie, let's go . . .

Frankie (*standing*) I'd better get him home.

Stephen It's your bet, Frankie.

Pause.

Frankie (*to* **Sweeney**) You OK? I mean . . .

Pause.

Sweeney No, you stay.

Frankie Cheers . . . I'm doing my money here, mate, sorry.

Frankie *sits down.*

Sweeney See you, guys.

Mugsy See you, Sween.

Carl Night, Sween.

Sweeney Nice to meet you, Ash, I hope you win the fucking lot. I'll see you, Stephen.

Stephen Sweeney, do you think you and Louise will manage to find somewhere with no entrance fees tomorrow? You could try the Tate Gallery . . . is she fond of Giacometti?

Beat.

I'll see you first thing, Tuesday, lunch. Sweeney?

Sweeney (*in tears*) Yeah.

Stephen Here you are . . . fifty quid . . . overtime.

He holds up a fifty-pound note.

Sweeney (*taking the note*) Cheers.

Frankie Sween . . .

Sweeney No.

Sweeney *exits.*

Beat.

Ash Your bet.

Frankie Yep.

Carl Eights or better?

Frankie Yep.

Mugsy The wheel goes?

Frankie Uh-huh.

Stephen With declarations?

Frankie Cards speak. I raise.

Scene Three

Later.

Ash *and* **Stephen** *are offstage.*

Mugsy So what exactly did you say to Stephen about the restaurant, Carl?

Carl I'm sorry, Mugs, I tried, he just wasn't interested.

Ash's mobile phone starts to ring.

Frankie Aye aye.

Frankie *removes the phone from* **Ash**'s *coat pocket. The phone continues to ring.*

Carl Don't, Frankie.

Frankie What? Might be important.

Carl It's not your phone.

Frankie All right, don't get your Y-fronts knotted, Carl.

Mugsy Go on, answer it.

Carl It's not your phone.

Mugsy Maybe something's happened, might be urgent.

Frankie Yeah and he gets called away with our money . . .

Frankie *gives the phone back to* **Carl** *as* **Stephen** *enters carrying a bottle of whisky.*

Stephen Did he have that thing in the restaurant?

Mugsy Yeah.

The phone stops ringing.

Stephen Well I hope it didn't go off in there, it specifically says on the menu, 'No Mobile Phones'.

Frankie What, might've disturbed the other customer?

Stephen Very funny, Frankie. Where's he gone?

Carl Cigarette, outside.

Mugsy Can't play poker if you ain't a smoker.

Frankie You don't smoke.

Beat.

Mugsy Yeah . . . I know . . . but if I did.

Frankie   Do you smoke, Carlton?

Carl   Me? No.

Frankie   I wonder why.

Stephen   Could it be because it kills you? Be my guest,
Frankie . . . outside. Actually, I've always thought it's a
rather interesting tell . . . smoking. Who wants to live, who
wants to die?

Mugsy   He's got a point.

Frankie   Judas.

Mugsy   Yeah, well, I'm pissed off with you chucking your
fag-ends in my saddle-bag.

Frankie (*to* **Stephen**)   Hard to believe you were a sixty-a-
day man.

Stephen   Forty. Your 'teacher' friend is rather good,
Carl . . .

Carl   He's just being lucky, that's all.

Frankie (*riffling his chips*)   I'll sort him out.

Stephen   Oooh, big man. How long did he teach you for?

Carl   Two years.

Stephen   Funny I never met him . . .

Carl   Probably because you never came to visit.

Stephen   Yes I did.

Carl   Twice, in five years.

He goes to the fridge.

Beer anyone? Frankie?

Frankie   Yeah, cheers.

Stephen   What did you say he taught you?

Carl   I didn't.

Stephen   So what did he teach you?

Carl   General Studies. Mugs?

Mugsy   Is there a Tango in there?

Carl   Yeah, your flat one from last week.

Mugsy   Yeah, give it here. I won last week, must be a lucky can.

Carl *gives* **Mugsy** *the can.*

Mugsy   I thought it was Economics?

Carl   As part of General Studies.

Stephen   Curiouser and curiouser.

Mugsy   Think Sween's OK?

Frankie   Yeah, he was a bit pissed that's all.

Stephen   Probably not used to such fine claret.

Frankie   Here you are . . . Fagin.

He throws eighty pounds in chips to **Stephen**.

Stephen   Thank you . . . Dodger. Actually, you can have a discount for prompt payment.

He throws him a five-pound chip.

Frankie   Isn't staff discount ten per cent?

Stephen   That's if you're still on the staff, Frankie.

Frankie   I might not be.

Ash *enters.*

Mugsy   Oi, mate, your mobile went off. It's OK though, we took a message, 'Give us the money or the kid gets it.'

Pause.

Carl   We let it ring.

Ash *sits down.*

Ash   Right. Hold 'em.

He begins to deal two down cards to each player.

Stephen   Ah, a man after my own heart.

Mugsy   Oi, Frankie, I forgot, what was she like?

Frankie Who?

Mugsy The bird last night.

Frankie Never you mind.

Carl Call.

Stephen I fail to understand what these women see in you.

Frankie Bit of rough, innit. Yep.

Mugsy Rough deemond. I'm in.

Frankie You should've seen him last night, he was well on the sniff.

Stephen I can assure you I was not 'on the sniff'. She looked like Miss Albania 1975. Call.

Ash No raise. The flop.

Ash *turns over three up cards.*

Frankie Stevie boy doesn't like women Ash, prefers to surround himself with virile younger men. All stems from this high-stakes poker game he got involved in, lost half his income to a woman, game called . . . Divorce. You ever played that?

Ash Yeah, but I won.

Frankie Resulto, what d'you win?

Ash My freedom. The flop is ace of clubs, four of clubs, seven of diamonds.

Mugsy Deemonds.

Carl Check.

Frankie So ever since then he's become a bit of a . . .

Stephen Oh, Frankie, and you were doing so well. The word you're groping for is –

Frankie I know the word, 'misogynist'.

Stephen That's the one.

Ash Your bet.

Frankie   Check.

Stephen   And how are you spelling 'misogynist'?

Beat.

No, OK, we'll come back to you.

Frankie   I'm spelling it with an F for fuck —

Stephen   Too late, Frankie, the moment's gone.

Ash   Your bet.

Mugsy   Me? Check.

Stephen   Check.

Ash (*dealing the next card*)   Eight of diamonds.

Mugsy   Deemonds.

Frankie   WILL YOU FUCKING SHUT UP ABOUT YOUR FUCKING DEEMONDS.

Pause.

Carl *knocks indicating check*, **Frankie** *knocks*, **Mugsy** *knocks*, **Stephen** *knocks*, **Ash** *knocks and then deals the final card*.

Ash   Ace of spades.

Carl *knocks*, **Frankie** *knocks*, **Mugsy** *knocks*.

Stephen   Ten.

Ash   Raise, thirty.

Carl   Pass.

Frankie   Pass.

Mugsy   Pass, the discipline of the man.

Stephen   Pass, I can't call.

Mugsy   Granite.

Stephen   No, real discipline, Mugs. Look, (*He turns over his cards.*) kings in the box, aces on the board — I can't call. What d'you have?

Ash *shows his cards.*

Stephen He bluffed me. Carl, will you get this man out of here, please.

Mugsy House rules, mate, no bluffing the management.

Ash I'll bear it in mind.

Stephen Carl, your deal.

Carl Five-card draw, red threes and black twos wild.

Mugsy Yes.

Stephen Oh, for God's sakes, Carl let's not play silly games.

Carl It's Dealer's Choice.

Stephen You can't play draw with wild cards, it's a classic game you can't 'customise' it.

Carl Fine, we'll play Hold'em all night.

Stephen Don't be pathetic.

Frankie If you're gonna play stupid kids' games I might as well go and play 'rummy' with my nan.

Stephen He's absolutely right.

Carl It's Dealer's Choice.

Mugsy 'Cept when Stephen and Frankie don't like it.

Frankie I'm going after the next hand.

Stephen Now look what you've done.

Carl I haven't done anything.

Stephen Look, we've played silly buggers all night, can we please play some serious poker with no wild cards. I'm going for a piss. Discuss.

Stephen *exits*.

Mugsy Frankie, don't go.

Frankie There's no skill involved with wild cards, it's all luck.

Mugsy And that's why you're going?

Frankie   Yeah.

Mugsy   No other reason you can think of? No? Cos it's just occurred to me that there might be another reason like for example the fact that for the first time in living memory you're actually losing.

Frankie   What and you're winning?

Mugsy   No, no I'm not, but at least I'm staying to the end, at least I'm a good loser.

Frankie   THAT'S WHY YOU'RE A LOSER. YOU MUG.

Pause.

Ash   Go on, Carl, deal a round of Hold'em while your dad's gone.

Carl   OK, Hold'em.

Carl *deals two down cards to each player.*

Mugsy   So what exactly did you say to him, Carl? Cos he didn't seem too keen, you were supposed to soften him up.

Carl   I did my best, Mugs, I'm sorry.

Frankie   Ten to play.

Mugsy   Pass.

Ash   Call.

Carl   Not for me. The flop . . .

He deals three cards up.

Three of hearts, king of clubs, jack of hearts.

Frankie   Fifty.

Ash   Call.

Carl *deals another card up.*

Carl   Ten of diamonds.

Beat.

Mugsy   Deemonds.

Frankie *looks at him.*

Frankie   Hundred.

Ash   Call.

Carl *deals the final up card.*

Carl   Nine of spades.

Beat.

Frankie   Four hundred and twenty-five, all in.

Ash   Call.

Pause.

I'm seeing you.

Pause.

Frankie   Nothing . . .

Ash   Pair of threes.

Ash *rakes in the chips.*

Frankie   How can you call with a pair of threes?

Ash   Fancied it.

Frankie   D'you see that, Mugs? He called four hundred with a pair of threes?

Mugsy   Play the man not the cards.

Beat.

Frankie   How d'you know?

Ash   Know what?

Frankie   That I was bluffing.

Ash   I guessed.

Frankie   You guessed for more than six hundred quid.

Ash   Guess so.

Frankie   Bollocks.

Carl   Frankie.

Frankie   Fuck off. How d'you know?

Beat.

Ash You've got a tell.

Frankie Me? What tell?

Ash That'd be telling.

Frankie Yeah, I ain't got a tell, you just tilted in like a mug.

Beat.

Ash D'you really want to know what your tell is?

Frankie Yeah.

Ash Sure?

Frankie Yes.

Beat.

Ash When you bluff you look scared.

Silence.

Who's deal?

Carl Frankie's . . .

Mugsy How much you up?

Ash I dunno, couple of grand.

Mugsy Nice. I expect you'll be doing a bit of investing with that quite soon?

Ash Yeah.

Mugsy Cos, you know I was telling you about this property in Mile End –

Frankie It's not a property it's a toilet.

Ash It's a toilet?

Mugsy It's an extremely large public convenience smack bang in the middle of the Mile End Road. It's thirties. Art deco.

Frankie Is it fuck.

Mugsy It would make a fantastic restaurant.

Frankie Bollocks.

Ash There are precedents.

Mugsy Are there?

Ash Sure.

Frankie Who the fuck are you?

Mugsy FRANKIE, I AM IN A BUSINESS MEETING. (*To* **Ash**.) What presidents?

Ash (*to* **Carl**) You know my snooker club, that used to be a toilet.

Carl Still is.

Mugsy I can have mine for a grand.

Ash Cheap.

Mugsy Yeah. D'you reckon it could work, something liked this but with a Frenchy/Italianey flavour in the Mile End neighbourhood?

Ash Yeah, I bet they're gagging for some of that in the Mile End neighbourhood.

Frankie *gets up from the table and puts on his coat.* **Stephen** *enters.*

Mugsy Would you come and have a look next week?

Ash Yeah, love to.

Mugsy Yeah, brilliant, I'll get your number off Carl. Thanks, thank you. I'll ring you tomorrow.

Ash Always here.

Stephen I'm frightfully sorry, have I interrupted a board meeting?

Mugsy Never you mind.

Stephen Whose deal? Frankie? Frankie?

Pause.

Frankie I'm out.

Frankie *exits.*

Mugsy   Right, my deal. Let's play . . . any requests?

Stephen   Hold'em.

Mugsy   Ash?

Ash   Omaha.

Mugsy   Let's play . . . a game for men of vision . . .
Omaha.

Scene Four

Later.

Ash   Call.

Mugsy   Trip sixes.

Ash   Sorry, mate, I've got a straight.

Mugsy   Yeah, I thought you might. Last card?

Ash   Yuh.

Ash *rakes in the chips.*

Stephen   Is that it, Mugs?

Mugsy   Yep, no more.

Carl   Bad luck, Mugs.

Mugsy   I've just been so unlucky.

Beat.

I've done a grand . . . I've done a fucking grand. Fuck.

Stephen   Mugs, go home, get some sleep.

Mugsy   Yeah. Listen, can I have a word with you,
Stephen, it's just . . . I . . . I've only got four hundred in cash
. . . I'm not sure whether my cheque . . .

Ash   I'm going for a smoke.

Mugsy   Sorry to break up the game.

Ash   That's all right. Carl.

Carl stands. **Ash** exits.

Mugsy Sorry, Carl, it's just –

Carl It's all right Mugs.

Carl exits.

Mugsy I'm sorry, I thought I was going to win so I'd be able to –

Stephen It's all right, Mugsy.

Mugsy I mean, can you dock it off my wages?

Stephen Yuh, it's fine.

Mugsy I'll do more overtime so I can –

Stephen I just said it's fine. We'll sort it out tomorrow.

Beat.

Mugsy, this restaurant of yours, how much did you and Carl want to borrow to secure the premises?

Mugsy A grand.

Beat.

Stephen One thousand pounds. You're sure?

Mugsy Course I'm fucking sure. Sorry. I do know how it sounds . . . a toilet in Mile End but it could've worked if you'd have . . .

Stephen You don't give up, do you? It's not easy, you know. Running a restaurant.

Mugsy No I know, I mean I don't know but –

Stephen Working with people like Sweeney and Frankie – Frankie, how would you deal with that?

Mugsy I wouldn't employ Frankie.

Stephen And now you're going to get this Ash 'character' to invest in you?

Mugsy He did say he'd come and have a look.

Stephen So he's your man?

Mugsy No, you were my first choice. You still are.

Stephen You should be careful, you know, Mugsy. I'm the businessman, I'm the restaurateur, I could take your idea, buy the premises tomorrow and cut you out like that.

Mugsy Yeah but you wouldn't. I trust you.

Stephen We're on the same level of circles?

Mugsy Words to that effect.

Enter **Carl** *and* **Ash**.

Carl OK?

Stephen Yes, come in, join the party, there must be so much to talk about.

Carl Yes. Listen, Mugsy . . . I've won . . . I can pay you, why don't I pay you the five hundred I owe you? Here . . . (*He stacks five hundred pounds in chips*.) thanks for the loan.

Mugsy Are you sure?

Carl Of course I'm sure, I owe it to you.

Mugsy Thanks, Carl.

Carl No problem.

Stephen Anyone else?

Carl Yeah, I was just about to. A hundred pounds as promised. Thanks, Dad.

He gives **Stephen** *one hundred pounds in chips*.

Stephen The Prodigal Son.

Mugsy Whose deal?

Stephen What?

Mugsy Whose deal?

Stephen It's over, Mugs, the game is over.

Mugsy Bollocks it is, I've got five hundred quid here.

Stephen Are you fucking mad?

Mugsy   No, are you scared, Stephen? Scared my luck's going to change? Come on, half an hour, come on . . . Carl?

Carl   I don't mind.

Mugsy   Ash?

Ash   Yeah, if you want.

Stephen   I'm not playing.

Mugsy   Why not?

Carl   Come on, Dad –

Stephen (*to* **Mugsy**)   Why can't you call it a night?

Mugsy   Because I want to win my money back.

Stephen   That's not the reason, it's you, you can't stop, it's no fun for you unless you lose.

Mugsy   I don't want to lose. Deal, Carl.

Stephen   Yes you do, you're addicted to it. You can't stop punishing yourself.

Mugsy   Deal, Carl.

Stephen   Mugsy, I'm trying to protect you.

Mugsy   From what?

Stephen   What do you think?

Mugsy   I don't know, what?

Stephen   From yourself.

Mugsy   I don't need protecting from myself, I'm my own best friend. I'm on my side.

Stephen   I'm on your side.

Mugsy   Bollocks, you're on your side, he's on his side, Carl's on his side, I'm on my side. Just deal. Someone. Please.

Carl   Hold'em.

Stephen   You're mad.

Mugsy   Yeah yeah.

Carl Hold'em, just for you, Dad.

Carl *deals two down cards to each player.*

Stephen   I'm out.

Mugsy   Half an hour, half an hour.

Stephen   Look at him, he's like a junkie with a new fix.
Correction, he *is* a junkie with a new fix.

Mugsy   Ten. Stephen.

Stephen   No.

Mugsy   Your bet.

Stephen   No.

Mugsy   Your bet.

Stephen   No.

Mugsy   Your bet.

Stephen   No.

Mugsy   Bet or pass. Bet or pass, Stephen.

Beat.

Stephen   Call.

Mugsy   Good man.

Ash   Call.

Mugsy   Good man.

Carl   Game on.

Mugsy   Coming to get you, boys, you know what the good
book says, 'early leaders, morning bleeders'. Flop 'em.

Carl *deals the flop.*

Mugsy   Deemonds.

Stephen   They're back.

Mugsy   Check.

Stephen   Forty.

Ash Pass.

Carl No.

Mugsy Gotcha. I call the forty and raise a hundred and twenty.

Stephen Got a good hand, Mugsy?

Mugsy Cashews and almonds, mate, otherwise known as 'the nuts'.

Stephen I call.

Mugsy Thus he enters the poker graveyard.

Carl Two of clubs.

Beat.

Stephen Coffin for Mr Mugsy?

Mugsy Check.

Stephen Not so nutty now, eh? How much have you got left?

Mugsy Three hundred and thirty.

Stephen That's the bet.

Mugsy I don't believe it. I've got top trips on the flop and then a fucking flush comes.

Stephen Tell you what, stick your tie in as well and we'll call it an even three fifty.

Mugsy The tie is worth thirty.

Stephen All right, three sixty. Come on, Mugs, stick your money in, lose the pot and bugger off home.

Mugsy (*taking off his tie*) Fuck it, call. Come on, on their backs, Stephen, there you go trip queens, what have you got?

Stephen No, I'll let you suffer.

Mugsy Don't fuck about, Stephen, on their backs.

Stephen No, Mugsy, you need to learn your lesson.

Carl Dad –

Stephen   Deal, Carl.

Mugsy   No, backs.

Carl   Dad, house rules.

Stephen   Just deal.

Mugsy   Backs.

Stephen   Deal.

Mugsy   Tell me what you've got.

Stephen   There's a card to come.

Carl   He must have the flush.

Mugsy   I know he must.

Stephen   Deal, Carl.

Mugsy   All right, pair the board, pair the fucking board.

Mugsy *starts to pray.* **Carl** *deals the final up card.*

Carl   Six of hearts.

Mugsy   NOOOOHH.

He falls to the floor.

Stephen (*throwing his cards in*)   You win, Mugs.

Mugsy   YES. Yes. The Mug is back. It's a miracle. What did you have, Stephen?

Stephen   Trip fours.

Mugsy   Trip fours, bottom trips and you raised? You're losing it, mate, you're cracking up.

He rakes in the chips.

It's what I always say Ash, this game is about stamina. It's about never say die even when you're dead. I have risen from the ashes like the proverbial dodo. I am resurrected, it took the Lord three days, the Mug one hand. Trip fours and he calls a back-raise on that flop . . . you've lost it, mate.

Stephen   Yes all right, Mugs.

Mugsy   You are on tilt mate and I am rolling, The Mug Is On A Roll. Whose deal?

Carl   Yours.

Mugsy   Right. I'm going for a dump. I may be gone some time. But when I return I shall take you boys so deeply to the cleaners you will never have to wash again.

Mugsy *exits and almost immediately re-enters, sniffing intently.*

Stephen   What's wrong?

Mugsy   Sorry, I thought I could smell something . . .

Stephen   What?

Mugsy   Fear, mate, fear.

Mugsy *exits.*

Ash   Round of Omaha while we're waiting? Carl.

Carl *begins to deal four cards down to each player.*

Stephen   Yeah, fine. How much are you up?

Ash   About three grand.

Stephen   Three? The magic number. Is that enough?

Ash   More is always welcome.

They look at their cards. **Ash**'s *mobile starts to ring.*

Stephen   Yours, I believe?

Ash *gets up.*

Stephen   Don't mind us.

Ash *exits with the phone.*

Stephen   Nice chap, don't you think? Shall we make him a regular?

Carl   I know what you did. That last pot Mugsy just 'won' . . . you lost on purpose. You never had trip fours.

Stephen   Yes I did.

Carl   I passed trip fours. You lost on purpose, why?

Stephen   Because . . .

Carl   Because you pitied Mugsy? So it's not even an honest game . . .

Stephen   Don't you talk to me about honesty, Carl.

Carl   You think you've done him a favour?

Stephen   Yes I do, I've made him happy.

Carl   And what if he found out?

Stephen   Well, he's not going to find out, is he?

Carl   You just gave him a grand.

Stephen   He needs it.

Carl   And this evening you made me feel like shit about a hundred quid.

Stephen   I've got a feeling we're talking about a little bit more than a hundred pounds, Carl . . .

Carl   But you did give me shit about a hundred quid.

Stephen   And?

Carl   How am I supposed to feel?

Stephen   You tell me.

Carl   I feel . . . why him? What have you got against me?

Stephen   Carl . . . no . . . it's not like that. Do you think I . . . don't you see? Mugsy can't survive . . . you're different, don't you see? You're a talented boy. It's totally different . . . you're my son.

Ash *enters.*

Ash   I've got to go. Now. It's urgent.

Stephen   Someone not done their homework?

Pause.

Ash   I've got to cash in.

Stephen   But we're in the middle of a hand.

Ash   Look, I've got a problem here . . . your son –

Stephen Scared? Come on . . . be a sport.

Carl Please, Ash.

Beat.

Ash OK, last hand. You want to play no limit?

Stephen Yeah, if you like.

Ash Great.

Stephen What do you think of Marx's theory of the inevitable decline of capitalism?

Ash Unlikely. Look at us.

Carl Omaha.

Stephen What about Utilitarianism?

Ash No, Omaha.

Stephen How much did you say you were up?

Ash About three grand.

Stephen Is three enough, Carl?

Carl Dad, let me explain, the original outlay –

Stephen Ten.

Carl The original –

Stephen TEN. Sir?

Ash Call ten.

Carl Pass.

He deals the flop.

King . . . jack . . . jack . . .

Stephen Check.

Ash Fifty.

Stephen Call.

Carl *deals the next up card.*

Carl Seven of clubs.

Stephen Check.

Ash Hundred.

Stephen (*to* **Carl**) Do you think I'm stupid?

Carl No.

Stephen Call.

Carl *deals the final up card.*

Carl Ace of hearts.

Stephen Check. How much do you owe him?

Carl What are you talking about?

Stephen Give me at least a modicum of respect.

Carl I don't owe anything.

Stephen DON'T LIE TO ME, CARL.

Beat.

Are you going to make a bet?

Ash Yeah, I'll make a bet. Five hundred.

Stephen Raise. There's your five and I raise one thousand and twenty-six, all in.

Beat.

Professor?

Beat.

One thousand and twenty-six.

Beat.

Yes?

Ash I'm thinking.

Stephen Think away.

Beat.

Ash Call. House of jacks.

Stephen House of kings.

Pause.

Oh dear.

He rakes in the chips.

Goodbye, Mr Chips.

Enter **Mugsy**.

Mugsy   Deal me in.

Stephen   Sorry, Mugs, game's over.

Mugsy   Yeah but . . .

Stephen   Game's over, Mugsy, everybody's far too tired.

Mugsy *makes chicken noises.*

Stephen   Yeah yeah.

Mugsy   Stephen?

Stephen   Mugsy.

Pause.

Mugsy   All right, if you can't take the punishment I will spare you but next time, no mercy.

Carl   You poker genius.

Stephen   Are you up now, Mugsy?

Mugsy   Hold on, let me count . . . I most certainly am . . . I am winning, I am winning . . . I am winning . . . seven quid. I feel like I've won seven million though. You've got to stick at this game, if you don't suffer you don't improve. Am I right, Ash? Ash?

Stephen   You're absolutely right and with your winnings you can even get yourself a cab home.

Mugsy   I'm going home in a limo mate, I'm flying home in a Lear jet. Only joking, I'm on my bike. How much you up, Stephen?

Stephen   Hard to say. I think I'm winning though.

Mugsy   See, he never loses. Carl?

Carl   I don't know.

Mugsy   Ash? Oi, Ashy boy? How much you up?

Pause.

Stephen   Mr Ash has just lost a very big pot.

Mugsy   Oh right, sorry, mate. You're still well up though aren't you? What a result, do you realise I shall not have to suffer another week of abuse in the kitchen. I shall laud it over Frankie and Sweeney as befits a winner.

Carl   Of seven quid.

Mugsy   It's not about amounts, young Carl, it's about winners and losers and we are winners. Oh, Ashy boy, I'll give you a ring tomorrow about the restaurant. I just had a thought actually, on the bog, if we gave it an oriental feel we could call it –

Ash   Why don't you fuck off.

Pause.

Stephen   Mugsy, go home.

Mugsy   Right, night, everyone. (*He checks his watch.*) Morning rather.

Carl   Mugsy . . . that pot you just won . . .

Beat.

Mugsy   What?

Carl *looks at* **Stephen**.

Carl   Here's your winnings.

He hands **Mugsy** *seven pounds.*

Mugsy   Oh yeah, cheers.

Stephen   Well played, Mugsy.

Mugsy   Class always tells, Stephen, in the end. See you.

Mugsy *exits.*

Stephen   Go and make some coffee, Carl.

Carl Dad, I'm sorry –

Ash Do what your dad says, Carl.

Stephen Black, no sugar.

Carl exits.

Beat.

Ash You played the hand well.

Stephen Thank you. Got any kids?

Ash No.

Stephen Do you want a drink?

Ash I don't.

Stephen Why not?

Ash I used to.

Beat.

Stephen So . . .

Ash He owes me four grand.

Stephen Oh, four was it. How?

Ash Gambling debt.

Stephen When?

Ash All this year, mainly poker but I lent him for roulette, blackjack, you name it.

Stephen Where did you meet?

Ash Casino.

Stephen Why?

Ash Why what?

Stephen Why lend him?

Ash Liked him, saw myself, that bollocks.

Stephen And he liked you . . .

Ash Look, I'm not here to talk about your son, he means nothing to me now. He was value.

Stephen Fellow compulsive gambler?

Ash I'm not a compulsive gambler, I do it for a living.

Stephen Sounds compulsive to me.

Ash No, you're wrong. You're the compulsive.

Stephen What?

Ash Yeah, anyway who cares? The point is I'm owed four grand and I'd very much appreciate it now.

Stephen I'm sure you would.

Ash Come on, you have to pay it.

Stephen What on earth for? My son owes it to you, get it off him.

Ash He hasn't got it. Come on, it's a debt, I owe this money.

Stephen What do you mean I'm a compulsive gambler?

Ash You're doing it now.

Beat.

You're like him, you need the action.

Stephen And you don't?

Ash I need the money.

Stephen You do this for a living, you must have money.

Ash I live in a fucking bedsit.

Stephen (*mock sympathy*)   Ahh.

Ash approaches.

Ash Give me the money.

Stephen Don't you come near me.

Ash (*close*)   Scared? Excited? Turned on?

Beat.

Stephen Fuck off.

Beat.

Ash *lifts his arm as if to strike* **Stephen**. **Stephen** *flinches*.

Ash Tell you what, I'll toss you for it.

Stephen What?

Ash I'll toss you for it, go on, the whole lot, four grand, I'll toss you for it.

Stephen You're out of your mind.

Ash Go on. You know you want to.

Stephen I most certainly do not.

Ash I think you do. You could clear the debt in one second. Be a hero. Live a little . . . for once in your fucking life. Go on.

Stephen No.

Ash Call.

Stephen No.

Ash Come on, call . . .

Stephen No.

Ash Call.

Stephen No.

Ash Call.

Stephen NO.

Ash CALL.

Stephen NO.

Ash CALL.

Stephen NO.

Ash CALL.

Stephen NO.

Ash CALL.

Stephen   NO.

Ash   CALL.

Stephen   NO.

Ash   CALL, YOU YELLOW CUNT.

Stephen   HEADS.

Ash *flips the coin, catches it and holds it in his clenched fist. Both men stare at the fist. Five seconds. Without revealing the coin **Ash** puts it back in his pocket.*

Ash   Four grand on the toss of a coin?

Pause.

Stephen   Take it.

Ash *goes to the chip box and counts the cash quickly.*

Stephen   How did you know?

Ash   It's my job.

*He holds up a bundle of cash to **Stephen**.*

Four grand, want to count?

Stephen   No . . . I trust you.

Ash   Right. I'm off then, thanks for the game.

Stephen   Where are you going?

Ash   Another game.

Stephen   It's the morning.

Ash   Yeah, must dash.

Stephen   This other game, is that where you owe the money?

Ash   Yeah.

Stephen   Are you the mug?

Pause.

Ash   I don't know.

Pause.

Hey . . . I'm sorry. About Carl.

Stephen   Thank you.

Ash   Bit like aces, kids, I suppose. You fall in love with them, you can't pass . . .

Stephen   Yuh . . . sometimes you have to.

Carl *enters.* **Ash** *looks at him.* **Ash** *exits.* **Carl** *puts the coffee on the table.*

Carl   Coffee.

Stephen   Thank you. See, you could still make a good waiter.

Carl   Ha Ha. Look, if you're going to give me a bollocking will you just do it please . . .

Stephen   Is that what this is to you? A bollocking. I'm not your headmaster.

Silence.

He looks into the chip box.

Look, all the money's gone, we've been robbed. Where can it be?

Carl   Well, presumably you gave it to Ash.

Beat.

Stephen   Yuh. Did I have any choice?

Carl   Yes, you could've said no. You didn't have to protect me. You don't have to always be there for me.

Stephen   I'm your father.

Carl   So?

Stephen   So . . . everything.

Beat.

Carl   Why won't you let me fail?

Stephen   I am, you're doing great.

Carl   There's nothing wrong with failure as long as it's on your own terms.

Stephen   There's your mother.

Carl   Why are you like this?

Stephen   I'm not *like* anything. This is what I *am*.

Pause.

Carl, I don't want you to end up like . . . Ash. Do you think he's happy?

Carl   I'm doing OK.

Stephen   You're doing nothing.

Carl   I'm doing fine.

Stephen   You're doing fuck all. You're a waste of life, Carl. Don't take this personally, I'm just making observations.

Beat.

You have lied to me for a whole year.

Carl   I'm sorry.

Stephen   You've been coming in here every Sunday night 'Hi, Dad' 'Bye, Dad' and then you've gone straight off to a casino to gamble thousands of pounds with another man.

Carl   And you're jealous . . .

Pause.

Stephen   God, don't you just love Mugsy? I mean, he's straight. For all his bull-headed stupidity, for all his relentless inability to recognise his own inadequacy, that man is psychotically alive.

Carl   Fuck you. What you mean is he's controllable. Fuck you.

Stephen   The worm has turned . . .

Carl   You can't stop, can you? Look at you with your pissy little poker game . . . which gives you the illusion of power.

I've played with real men for real money. Ash lost every penny he ever had in one night.

Stephen The object of the game is to win.

Beat.

Carl You don't understand.

Stephen Yes I do.

Carl *goes to exit and then turns.*

Pause.

Carl Same time next week?

Stephen *looks at him. Long silence.*

Carl Night.

Carl *exits.*

Pause.

Stephen *sits at his desk and turns on the computer. The screen flashes into life revealing graphs and charts. He stares at the screen.*

Slow fade.

Methuen Modern Plays

include work by

Jean Anouilh

John Arden

Margaretta D'Arcy

Peter Barnes

Sebastian Barry

Brendan Behan

Edward Bond

Bertolt Brecht

Howard Brenton

Simon Burke

Jim Cartwright

Caryl Churchill

Noël Coward

Sarah Daniels

Nick Dear

Shelagh Delaney

Claire Dowie

David Edgar

Dario Fo

Michael Frayn

John Godber

Paul Godfrey

David Greig

John Guare

Peter Handke

David Hare

Jonathan Harvey

Iain Heggie

Declan Hughes

Terry Johnson

Sarah Kane

Charlotte Keatley

Robert Lepaga & Ex Machina

Stephen Lowe

Doug Lucie

Martin McDonagh

John McGrath

David Mamet

Patrick Marber

Arthur Miller

Mtwa, Ngema & Simon

Tom Murphy

Phyllis Nagy

Peter Nichols

Joseph O'Connor

Joe Orton

Louise Page

Joe Penhall

Luigi Pirandello

Stephen Poliakoff

Franca Rame

Philip Ridley

Reginald Rose

Willy Russell

Jean-Paul Sartre

Sam Shepard

Wole Soyinka

Theatre de Complicite

Theatre Workshop

Sue Townsend

Judy Upton

Timberlake Wertenbaker

Tennessee Williams

Victoria Wood

Methuen Contemporary Dramatists
include

Peter Barnes (three volumes)
Sebastian Barry
Edward Bond (six volumes)
Howard Brenton
  (two volumes)
Richard Cameron
Jim Cartwright
Caryl Churchill (two volumes)
Sarah Daniels (two volumes)
Nick Darke
David Edgar (three volumes)
Ben Elton
Dario Fo (two volumes)
Michael Frayn (two volumes)
Paul Godfrey
John Guare
Peter Handke
Jonathan Harvey
Declan Hughes
Terry Johnson (two volumes)
Bernard-Marie Koltès
David Lan
Bryony Lavery
Doug Lucie
David Mamet (three volumes)

Martin McDonagh
Duncan McLean
Anthony Minghella
  (two volumes)
Tom Murphy (four volumes)
Phyllis Nagy
Anthony Nielsen
Philip Osment
Louise Page
Joe Penhall
Stephen Poliakoff
  (three volumes)
Christina Reid
Philip Ridley
Willy Russell
Ntozake Shange
Sam Shepard (two volumes)
Wole Soyinka (two volumes)
David Storey (three volumes)
Sue Townsend
Michel Vinaver (two volumes)
Michael Wilcox
David Wood (two volumes)
Victoria Wood

Methuen World Classics
include

Jean Anouilh (two volumes)
John Arden (two volumes)
Arden & D'Arcy
Brendan Behan
Aphra Behn
Bertolt Brecht (six volumes)
Büchner
Bulgakov
Calderón
Čapek
Anton Chekhov
Noël Coward (seven volumes)
Eduardo De Filippo
Max Frisch
John Galsworthy
Gogol
Gorky
Harley Granville Barker
   (two volumes)
Henrik Ibsen (six volumes)
Lorca (three volumes)

Marivaux
Mustapha Matura
David Mercer (two volumes)
Arthur Miller (five volumes)
Molière
Musset
Peter Nichols (two volumes)
Clifford Odets
Joe Orton
A. W. Pinero
Luigi Pirandello
Terence Rattigan
   (two volumes)
W. Somerset Maugham
   (two volumes)
August Strindberg
   (three volumes)
J. M. Synge
Ramón del Valle-Inclán
Frank Wedekind
Oscar Wilde

Methuen Student Editions

John Arden	*Serjeant Musgrave's Dance*
Alan Ayckbourn	*Confusions*
Aphra Behn	*The Rover*
Edward Bond	*Lear*
Bertolt Brecht	*The Caucasian Chalk Circle*
	Life of Galileo
	Mother Courage and her Children
Anton Chekhov	*The Cherry Orchard*
Caryl Churchill	*Top Girls*
Shelagh Delaney	*A Taste of Honey*
John Galsworthy	*Strife*
Robert Holman	*Across Oka*
Henrik Ibsen	*A Doll's House*
Charlotte Keatley	*My Mother Said I Never Should*
John Marston	*The Malcontent*
Willy Russell	*Blood Brothers*
August Strindberg	*The Father*
J. M. Synge	*The Playboy of the Western World*
Oscar Wilde	*The Importance of Being Earnest*
Tennessee Williams	*A Streetcar Named Desire*
Timberlake Wertenbaker	*Our Country's Good*

Methuen Film *titles include*

The Wings of the Dove
Hossein Armini

Mrs Brown
Jeremy Brock

Persuasion
Nick Dear after Jane Austen

The Gambler
Nick Dear after Dostoyevsky

Beautiful Thing
Jonathan Harvey

Little Voice
Mark Herman

The Long Good Friday
Barrie Keeffe

The Crucible
Arthur Miller

The English Patient
Anthony Minghella

Twelfth Night
Trevor Nunn after Shakespeare

The Krays
Philip Ridley

The Reflecting Skin & The Passion of Darkly Noon
Philip Ridley

Trojan Eddie
Billy Roche

Sling Blade
Billy Bob Thornton

The Acid House
Irvine Welsh